The GARDEN BIRD Handbook

This edition first published in 2006 by New Holland Publishers (UK) Ltd
London • Cape Town • Sydney • Auckland
www.newhollandpublishers.com

2 4 6 8 10 9 7 5 3

Garfield House, 86-88 Edgware Road, London W2 2EA, United Kingdom

80 McKenzie Street, Cape Town 8001, South Africa

Unit 1, 66 Gibbes Street, Chatswood, NSW 2067, Australia

218 Lake Road, Northcote, Auckland, New Zealand

All photography by David M. Cottridge, with the exception of those listed on page 160

All artwork by David Daly, with the exception of those listed on page 160

ISBN 13: 978 1 84537 598 0

Publishing Manager: Jo Hemmings
Project Editor: Lorna Sharrock
Editorial Assistant: Gareth Jones
Copy Editor: Tim Sharrock
Designer: Alan Marshall
Assistant Designer: Gulen Shevki
Index: Janet Dudley
Production: Joan Woodroffe

Back cover: Redwing
Page 1: Marsh Tit
Page 3: Wood Pigeons
Pages 4-5: from top left: Barn Owl, Fieldfare, Blue Tit, Jay, garden with Buddleia flowering

Reproduction by Modern Age Repro Co. Ltd., Hong Kong
Printed and bound in Malaysia by Times Offset (M) Sdn Bhd

THE
wildlife
TRUSTS

The GARDEN BIRD Handbook

Stephen Moss

NEW HOLLAND

CONTENTS

The Wildlife Trusts

The Wildlife Trusts partnership is the UK's leading voluntary organization working, since 1912, in all areas of nature conservation. We are most fortunate to have the support of more than 600,000 members – people who care about British wildlife.

We protect wildlife for the future by managing almost 2,500 nature reserves across the UK, ranging from wetlands and peat bogs, to heaths, coastal habitats, woodlands and wildflower meadows. These habitats are home to Britain's birds from the rare Bittern and Manx Shearwater, to the endearing Puffin, Skylark and Barn Owl.

Left and above: *Birdbaths (left) and birdfeeders, such as this tit-bell (above), are two of a wide variety of ways to attract birds into your garden.*

The Garden Bird Handbook is a comprehensive guide to attracting, identifying and watching garden birds. The author, Stephen Moss, has provided sections covering basic to advanced bird gardens, a beautifully illustrated bird directory, practical tips on pest management, information on bird behaviour and the bird year.

Few realize just how endangered much of our British wildlife is. In recent years once common bird species have declined – including the Song Thrush and House Sparrow – and gardens are becoming increasingly important wildlife habitats.

The Wildlife Trusts works with Government, planners, companies and the public, to protect our wildlife for the future. Importantly, we encourage people to 'do their bit' for wildlife – and with the help of *The Garden Bird Handbook*, conservation can start at home!

Increasingly gardens are becoming a lifeline for birds and other wildlife. Across the UK we look after more than two million acres of garden – an area five times the size of Greater London. Our work has taken us to RHS Shows and even to No. 10 Downing Street, where the Prime Minister Tony Blair invited The Wildlife Trusts to build a wildlife pond just outside the cabinet room.

Your local Wildlife Trust will have information on nature reserves and wildlife activities, including wildlife gardening and dawn chorus events.

The Wildlife Trusts believes that it is not too late, that we all have a part to play in reversing the losses of the past, and ensuring that the UK really is a better place for wildlife and people. Help us to protect wildlife for the future and become a member today! Please phone The Wildlife Trusts on 0870 036 7711, or log on to www.wildlifetrusts.org for further information.

Thank you for buying *The Garden Bird Handbook* – we hope you have fun discovering the birds in your garden!

The Wildlife Trusts is a registered charity (number 207238).

Introduction

Watching garden birds is a more popular pastime than football and fishing. Two out of three people in Britain do it at last once a week. If you've bought, borrowed or been given this book, you are already on the way to joining them.

Taking an interest in garden birds

Feeding birds in the garden is one of the most popular pastimes in the country. It can be done by anyone, of whatever age, wherever they live, and without even knowing much about the birds themselves. It brings pleasure, fascination and joy to millions of people and, most importantly of all, it provides a vital lifeline for the birds themselves.

TV presenter, author and urban wildlife guru Chris Baines has described private gardens as 'Britain's biggest nature reserve', and he's right. They are also one of our most important ecological assets, yet until recently they have been mostly ignored by naturalists and conservationists, who seem to prefer the more glamorous habitats and rarer species.

Now, all that has changed. At the turn of the new millennium, it began to become clear that the British countryside was mostly devoid of wildlife. As a result of a combination of high-yield farming methods, road building and mismanagement of land, much of rural Britain is a sterile desert from a wildlife point of view. Today, even common species such as Starling, Song Thrush and House Sparrow are under threat.

Left: A large seed feeder will attract a wide range of species, including finches and tits.

Above: Wrens are our commonest bird and are found in most gardens. They are not always easy to see due to their small size.

Right: Blackcaps are an increasingly common garden visitor, especially in winter, when they often feed on berries.

In a desert, you need oases: and that's what our gardens are. Desperate for food, water and places to shelter and nest, our wildlife has come in from the countryside to seek shelter and sustenance in our gardens. Whether you live in a rural, suburban or urban area, the chances are that your garden has more birds and other wildlife living there than in the surrounding 'countryside'. Moreover, birds are breeding at higher densities, and producing more young, in gardens than almost anywhere else.

Above: *Song Thrushes love snails, which they extract from the shell by bashing them on a hard surface, known as its anvil, such as a garden patio or wall!*

Below: *Siskins were once rare garden birds, but in recent years they have become regular visitors to many gardens throughout the country.*

This is where *you* come in. By planting the right mix of trees, shrubs and flowering plants; by adding a feature such as a pond; by putting up nestboxes; and, most important of all, by providing a reliable, regular supply of food and water; you will be contributing to the survival of some of our best-known and best-loved birds. At the same time, you'll be helping other, less visible wildlife such as hedgehogs, moths and frogs. In addition, you'll get a whole lot of enjoyment out of it. So, don't be shy: join the club!

A history of garden bird feeding

According to the great twentieth-century ornithologist James Fisher, the first recorded instance of man feeding birds was St Serf of Fife, who during the sixth century AD tamed a Robin, which would come to his hand for food. Fisher believed that the habit of sharing meagre supplies of food with birds continued throughout the Dark Ages, and that, by Victorian times, it was taken for granted as a social ritual. Indeed, the nicknaming of postmen as 'Robins' and the appearance of the Robin on Christmas cards during the late Victorian era indicates a close relationship between man and birds.

At the same time, in Germany, Baron Von Berlepsch of Schloss Seebach became obsessed with the notion that, by feeding wild birds, and providing places for them to nest, you could control insect pests: organic gardening a century before its time!

By the time that Fisher was writing, in the 1960s, he described garden-bird feeding as 'big business', while another ornithologist, Richard Fitter, estimated that, during the Big Freeze of 1962/63, 'the housewives of Britain may have saved the lives of at least a million birds.' He listed 40 species that will come to garden birdfeeders; today's count is well over 100. One major change since Fisher's day is that he described the Siskin as 'so far almost unknown at feeders,' whereas now it is a common and regular visitor to many gardens.

During the 1990s, a combination of sustained effort from The Wildlife Trusts, the RSPB and the British Trust for Ornithology (BTO), especially their Garden BirdWatch scheme (see *Garden Bird Behaviour*); and the arrival on the scene of new and dynamic bird-food suppliers, such as Haith's and

C.J. Wildbird Foods, combined to raise the profile of garden-bird feeding. Even BBC Radio's venerable *Today* programme got in on the act, giving publicity to the RSPB's 'Big Garden Birdwatch' scheme.

Today, feeding garden birds has never been more popular. Hence the need for this book.

How to use this book

The Garden Bird Handbook attempts to give a comprehensive account of the process of attracting, watching and identifying the birds that visit your garden. It consists of eight chapters, which aim to cover all aspects of making your garden as attractive to the birds as possible, and helping you to get the most out of it. These are:

- **The Key Elements**: an overview of what you will need to do to attract birds to your garden.
- **Gardens for Birds**: three proposed approaches, from a basic bird garden, requiring the minimum of expense and effort, to an advanced bird garden.
- **Understanding Garden Bird Behaviour**: a guide to the various common and unusual types of behaviour that you may encounter when watching your garden birds.
- **The Garden Bird Year**: a month-by-month account of the comings and goings of birds during the year.
- **Troubleshooting**: a guide to dealing with problems such as pests and predators.
- **Identifying Birds in your Garden**: an illustrated guide to 50 common species, 30 less-usual visitors, and birds that might fly over your garden, with hints and tips on how to identify them, and other useful information.
- **Plants to Attract Birds**: a selection of plant types and species that you may wish to consider and their uses for the birds.

No book can tell you everything that you need to know. I hope, however, that I can show you the basic steps that you need to take, help you to solve one or two identification puzzles and, most important of all, inspire you to create a garden fit for a variety of birds to live in. Good luck!

Above: *Blackbirds love feeding on open lawns, where they can often find a juicy earthworm or two! This bird has a fight on its hands as it tries to extract the worm from the soil.*

Below: *Fruit trees such as the apple provide blossom in spring that attracts plenty of insects such as flies, butterflies and bees. Insects, in turn, attract birds to your garden. Try to choose native varieties of trees if you can, although some non-native species do attract insects too.*

The Key Elements

If you want to be successful at attracting birds into your garden – and keeping them there – there are a number of key elements that you simply must provide. In roughly descending order of importance, these are: food, water, nesting sites, and shelter and safety.

Food and feeders

Birds must eat, or they will die. By providing a regular, reliable and nutritious supply of food, throughout the year, you will do a great deal to help birds survive and reproduce, thus benefiting not just the birds in your garden today, but future generations too. For example, a Blue Tit weighing about 8–10 grams needs between 2–3 grams of food every day to survive.

You'll also find that, once the birds get to know that there is food available, they make a point of stopping off in your garden on their circuit around the neighbourhood. In turn, the presence of a few birds will attract more, and before you know it you'll be running a dawn-to-dusk fast-food restaurant for the birds.

You can also help by providing sources of natural food such as seed- and berry-bearing plants, or those that attract insects. Choose a variety of mostly native plants, as these are generally more suited to providing food.

Water: baths and ponds

For many species, especially those that eat dry foods such as seeds, water is almost as important as food itself. A birdbath will soon become a focal point of any bird garden, as it provides a reliable supply of fresh, clean water for drinking and bathing. This is especially important during summer droughts or winter freezes, when alternative supplies may be hard to find. A garden pond is also a key element, as it will attract a far wider variety of birds as they come to feed, drink and bathe.

Left: *The Robin is one of our best-known and best-loved garden birds. In winter, they often feed on juicy berries, which provide much-needed energy, especially during prolonged periods of ice and snow when other food is scarce.*

Above and right: *You can help the birds in your garden by providing places to nest such as a nestbox for a Great Tit and its brood (above), and a birdbath for birds such as this Feral Pigeon (right).*

Above: Although they usually prefer to feed on berries, the rare Waxwing will occasionally feed on fruit on the ground such as windfall apples.

Below: The Spotted Flycatcher can be found in large, rural gardens with plenty of flowering plants to attract the insects that it feeds on. It is a summer visitor to Europe, arriving in May and remaining until August or early September.

Nesting and nestboxes

The point of being a bird – as with any other living creature – is to reproduce: to raise a family and pass on their genes to a new generation. For small birds such as Robins and Wrens this is truly vital: if they fail to breed this year they may not get the chance again, as their average life expectancy is pitifully short.

As with food, you can help in two ways: by planting shrubs, bushes and trees to provide natural nest sites, and by putting up nestboxes. This is easier than it sounds: basic nestbox designs can now be bought for less than £10 each and will, if looked after, last for many years. It is also quite simple to make your own nestbox (see page 30).

Shelter and safety

Birds need places to rest, especially at night, when many species roost together for warmth and safety. You can help, both by providing plenty of natural foliage, and also by making your garden as safe as possible for the birds you attract there. Sometimes, you may feel you are fighting a losing battle, especially if your garden is a haven for cats and Magpies. But don't despair, there are ways of deterring even the most determined predator. Disease is another potential killer, so hygiene and cleanliness are important, especially in feeding areas.

Enjoyment

This final element is more about you and your family than the birds. There is simply no point in spending time, money and effort providing a five-star service for your garden birds if you are not going to get something back. So, as you plan your bird garden, think about designing it for your benefit as well as for that of the birds. As well as making sure the birdtables, feeders and nestboxes are in the correct place for the birds' benefit, check that you can see them too – from your favourite birdwatching spot (possibly a garden bench or your kitchen window). Then sit back and enjoy a show to rival the world's greatest natural history spectacles: stunning close-up views of real birds enjoying the benefits of something that you have created. Better than wildlife programmes on television any day!

Food and Feeders

There are three main reasons why you should feed birds in your garden. First, it helps individual birds to survive and makes their lives a little bit easier. Secondly, at a time when populations of many common species are declining, it may help halt or even reverse the trend, by providing a sanctuary for them. Last, and certainly not least, feeding your garden birds will bring you, your family and your friends immense pleasure and enjoyment throughout the year.

In winter, birds need food to survive: without the energy that it provides, they simply will not live long enough to breed the following year. However, even in the spring and summer, they still need your help: when feeding hungry young, the adults may fail to find enough food for themselves. So, if you have decided to provide food for your garden birds, make sure that you keep it up all year around.

The main reason that birds cannot just get food somewhere else is because post-war agricultural policies have turned much of our beloved countryside into a sterile desert, with virtually nothing left for the birds to eat. As a result, many have turned to gardens, and the food that we provide, in order to survive.

Feeding garden birds

These days, just about everybody feeds garden birds. Surveys have shown that more than two out of three of us now regularly put out food for the birds, and feeding garden birds has become a lucrative business opportunity for a few far-sighted entrepreneurs, who now supply everything you need by mail order straight to your doorstep.

Every year, it is estimated that we provide roughly 15,000 tonnes of peanuts: more than 30 *billion* individual nuts. And that's not to mention the vast amount of seeds and other foodstuffs that we also hand out. Yet, compared with the United States, we are mere beginners: the

Above: *Blue Tits regularly come to artificial feeders such as this hanging basket filled with peanuts. Feeding garden birds provides them with the energy they need to get through late autumn, winter and early spring.*

Americans spend more than 2 billion dollars (£1.4 billion) on bird feeding every year.

How to feed garden birds

There are two main ways to provide food for birds in your garden. First, by planting a range of bushes, shrubs and trees that in turn provide berries and fruit, or which attract insects, for the birds to feed on (for more details see *Plants to Attract Birds*). Secondly, by providing a range of different foods, at different levels, using different delivery systems, all designed to attract the widest variety of species and largest number of individual birds to your garden.

Once you have started providing food, it is essential that you keep up a regular supply, as birds will make regular visits on their feeding circuits. But don't overstock your feeders and birdtable: not only will it be a waste of

money, but you may attract pests such as rats and mice, or cause food poisoning in the birds themselves.

You don't need to provide a five-star service straight-away. Even a single seed dispenser or peanut feeder will begin to attract birds and you can add a wider range of food and feeders later.

Where you buy your food is important. Avoid buying loose, unlabelled food from pet shops or market traders: it may be poor quality or contaminated, or both. Approved providers such as the RSPB, or the various mail-order suppliers, are excellent and some garden centres also sell good-quality foodstuffs.

Basic feeders and foods

So, where do you start? The first step is to put up two or three simple birdfeeders, each providing a different type of food. These start off at under £5, although larger models may cost from £10 up to £30. It's also worth considering

Left: *Leaving part of your garden to 'go wild' will provide plenty of seeds, as well as attracting a whole host of insects on which the birds can feed.*

Below left and right: *To attract a wide range of birds, it is worth experimenting with a range of different food and feeders. This Nuthatch (left) prefers peanuts, while the pair of Great Tits (right) use their acrobatic skills to get at the fat stored underneath the tit-bell.*

Above: *The roof of this hanging birdtable will prevent the food getting wet in the rain, and the hanging design will discourage unwanted visitors such as rats and squirrels.*

Above: *Seeds are packed with energy, so the birds need to use less effort to get enough food to survive. Birds become highly skilled at getting seeds from specially-designed dispensers.*

metal rather than plastic feeders. Although they cost a few pounds more, they are generally sturdier and will last much longer against the weather.

Feeders come in two main kinds: wire mesh for peanuts, and tubular plastic ones for seeds. They have little perches allowing the birds to feed more easily at each opening.

Peanuts used to be the staple diet of our garden birds, but in recent years two things have reduced their popularity. First, some supplies have been found to be contaminated with a substance called aflatoxin, which poisons the birds. Secondly, although fine as a basic food, peanuts do not contain as much energy as sunflower seeds. When you provide both seeds and peanuts, you tend to find that the birds prefer the seeds, especially if you have bought premium varieties such as sunflower hearts. These have little or no wastage and a very high oil content, making them excellent for building up energy.

Although it may seem expensive at first, it is worth considering buying peanuts and seeds in bulk: there are usually substantial savings to be made. Once bought, store them in a cool, dry place, preferably in a plastic box or bin to keep out mice.

You can hang your feeders from a tree, post or birdtable, or place them freestanding on a pole, which may deter rats, cats and squirrels. Experiment with a range of different positions and methods, until you find the one that the birds seem to prefer.

If you have a problem with squirrels, you may want to invest in a 'squirrel-proof' feeder: basically a wire-mesh peanut holder enclosed in a 'cage', which allows small birds such as tits to get in, but excludes larger birds, squirrels and cats. The main problem with these is that small birds may be reluctant to enter what appear to be the bars of a cage.

Above: *In recent years, bird food manufacturers have developed a range of specialist foods, including this special bar containing high energy fat, seeds and even insects!*

Specialist foods

After a while, you may want to experiment with more exotic and unusual foods in order to attract a wider range of bird species. You can start with specialist seeds such as niger (or nyger), a small black variety of sunflower seed that Goldfinches seem to love.

Food bars or cakes are also excellent: they are made of high-energy fat (sometimes with added insects), and are designed to attract insect-eaters such as Robins and Blackcaps.

Mealworms and waxworms are also excellent: although quite expensive there is virtually no waste and Robins, Dunnocks and Jays love them. Just put them out in a smooth-sided bowl to prevent escape,and watch the birds come. Mealworms can be bought by mail order from specialist bird-food dealers, but don't tell your postman what is in the parcel!

VARIETY OF FOODS SUITABLE FOR BIRDS

Below: *The key to attracting the widest possible range of species into your garden is to provide a good range of foods.*

Bread and cooked rice attract a wide range of species, including Starlings.

Peanuts and seeds attract tits, finches and sparrows, along with many other small birds.

Apples are excellent for thrushes such as the Blackbird.

Sunflower seeds are full of energy, ideal for all small birds such as tits and finches.

A variety of other seeds is available to suit specialist feeders such as the Goldfinch.

The birdtable

A bird garden without a birdtable is like a theatre without a stage. It provides a centrepiece, allowing you to provide a wider variety of foods, and in turn attracts a range of species that rarely come to feeders.

A well-designed table should have a sturdy central pole, which is either freestanding or designed to be sunk into the ground. It should also have a roof to keep out rain and snow, though some tables are so badly designed that the roof will not allow larger birds to gain access. In my view, the best tables have a large feeding platform that is only partly covered by the roof; perhaps even with a removable roof so that you can take it off completely in fine weather.

You can either buy your birdtable, or make it yourself. Prices for ready-made ones range from around £20, for the most basic models, to almost £100 for bigger, sturdier ones. Making it yourself should save you a few pounds, but may take a fair amount of skill and effort.

Whether you make or buy, make sure that the pole is strong enough to support the weight of the table (plus

Above: *A birdtable should be the centrepiece of every bird-friendly garden. It allows you to provide a variety of different foods to attract different species.*

food). Once you have your table, try placing it in several different positions in the garden to discover which the birds prefer. Don't be impatient, however: birds will always take a few days to get used to a birdtable and may at first seem reluctant to use it.

The great thing about a birdtable is that it allows you to provide a far wider variety of foodstuffs than before. You can put out loose seed, kitchen scraps and leftovers, stale bread, fruit such as apples or raisins, even grated cheese or pet food. However, avoid feeding birds with hard-to-digest food such as uncooked rice or very stale bread. You can also hang your seed and peanut feeders from hooks.

Whatever food you put out, make sure that you clean up uneaten food every day or two, and keep the table clean by giving it a good scrub with soap and water every couple of weeks or so. By doing that, you will avoid the risk of disease or attracting vermin.

Should you feed all year around?

Until quite recently, most people who fed their garden birds stopped doing so sometime in late winter or early spring, and started up again in the autumn. Recent research has shown, however, that, as well as the winter period, when birds may starve to death because of lack of natural food, there is another critical period in the spring.

Once birds have chicks to feed, the need to find food is paramount. Most songbirds feed their young on invertebrates such as caterpillars and grubs, but in doing so they often find it hard to get enough food for themselves. So, by continuing to provide food throughout the breeding season (especially early on when natural food is scarce), you will be helping them to maintain critical energy levels.

By mid-summer, you can begin to reduce the food supply, as there is plenty of natural food for the birds to eat. Start increasing the quantity of food sometime during the autumn, usually about the time of the first frosts when natural food is becoming scarce again.

In winter, watch the weather forecast and, as soon as there is a spell of freezing weather, especially if it brings snow, make sure that you increase the amount of food on offer. You are sure to see an increase in numbers or birds and intensity of activity, and may see a few shyer species such as woodpeckers and Nuthatch coming to feed.

Water: Baths and Ponds

Birds need water for two main reasons: to drink and to bathe. You should, therefore, provide a water supply in the form of a birdbath (or two), which will enable the various different species that visit your garden to take advantage of a reliable and regular source. Another way to provide a permanent source of water is to build a garden pond, which – however small – will soon become a magnet for the birds. Another advantage of a garden pond is that it also attracts a huge range of other wildlife, including insects and other invertebrates for the birds to eat.

Choosing and siting a birdbath

After a birdtable and feeders, a birdbath is the next most essential piece of equipment in your garden. Choose a fairly simple design, without too many fancy features, which just get in the birds' way. A large bath is better than a small one, but make sure that it is not too deep, as this will deter smaller birds. Ideally, a birdbath should have a 'shallow end' and a 'deep end', so that it can be used by tits and finches

Below: *Starlings are frequent visitors to birdbaths, often arriving in flocks and taking turns to bathe, or shoving each other out of the way to be first in the queue!*

as well as by pigeons and doves. The surface should be fairly rough, to prevent slipping.

Put your birdbath on a stand, place it on the ground, or sink it into the earth. Make sure, however, that it is placed somewhere difficult for non-avian predators to gain access, or you will be providing a free meal for them.

You can buy your birdbath from the RSPB, a reputable supplier, or your local garden centre. Prices start at about £10 and go up to more than £50 for more ornate models. As with a new feeder, the birds will take a while to get used to the bath; but it should soon become a regularly used feature. If your budget cannot run to a birdbath use a shallow bowl, which you should embed into the ground to keep it secure and avoid water spillage.

Change the water in your birdbath every day or two, to stop the formation of algae and bacteria that cause disease. Clean the bath regularly (every week or two), using a hard scrubbing brush, soap and water (but make sure you rinse it thoroughly afterwards). In winter, especially when the temperature drops below 0°C due to a hard frost, make sure that you keep the water in your birdbath ice-free. The best way to do this is to add a kettle or saucepan full of boiling water once or twice a day; it will cool quickly for the birds to drink from it.

Above right: *A wide variety of bird species, including tits, will come to drink and bathe at a well-placed birdbath. This one is well established and is made more attractive by having moss growing over its base.*

Right: *Wood Pigeons are amongst many species to be attracted by a garden pond. Ponds provide an opportunity for larger birds such as pigeons and doves to drink and bathe.*

Planning a garden pond

Although it may seem a lot of hard work and effort, creating a pond in your garden really will bring benefits for the birds, as well as for a whole host of other wildlife. A well-planned, well-made pond provides a reliable supply of clean, fresh water for birds to drink and to bathe in; attracts insects and other creepy-crawlies, which provide a plentiful food resource; and will soon become an attractive feature in your garden.

Planning and making a pond does take effort, but perhaps not as much as you would think. A medium-sized pond (say 3-5 square metres) should take two or three people a weekend to make. The initial investment (for the pond liner and plants) may seem high, but you will be amazed at how quickly you reap the benefits. Within a few months, your pond will look as if it has been there for years. Do bear in mind, however, that, as well as the initial work, you will have to spend some time maintaining your pond, to get the best from it.

Siting your pond

Deciding where to put your pond may be difficult. Ideally, it should be at a low point of your garden, but not somewhere so boggy that the surroundings turn into a quagmire. A sunny, southerly or westerly aspect is ideal, as ponds need sunlight to help the plants grow. It should also be within sight of the house, so that you can enjoy the antics of the birds and other wild creatures that visit it.

It is best to avoid constructing a pond directly under a tree, otherwise leaves may fall in and rot (polluting the pond) and the pond may be too shaded, preventing many plants from thriving.

Once you have chosen the site, you will need to decide on the shape. Ideally, you should avoid a square or rectangular shape and go for something that looks a bit more natural. If you can, mark out the proposed shape with poles or a length of hose, and spend a few days varying it until you reach your preferred shape. Once you start digging, there is no going back!

FEATURES OF A WILDLIFE POND

Below: *A garden pond with the key features can transform your garden, attracting a wider variety of species than before. It may take a bit of effort, but it will be worthwhile.*

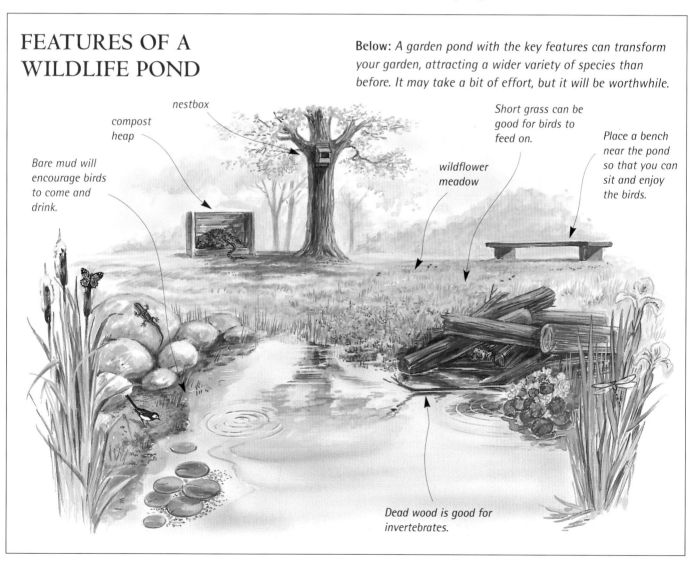

nestbox

compost heap

Short grass can be good for birds to feed on.

Place a bench near the pond so that you can sit and enjoy the birds.

Bare mud will encourage birds to come and drink.

wildflower meadow

Dead wood is good for invertebrates.

Making your pond

Making a garden pond requires military-style planning. Choose a fine weekend, ideally in autumn, before the frost has made the ground too hard to dig. You can make your pond as late as March, though in the depths of winter the daylight hours are short and the ground may be frozen.

The right equipment is also essential. You will need a range of spades and at least one wheelbarrow to remove the soil, and a tape measure and calculator to measure the proposed hole and work out the size of lining required. The lining should be flexible, ideally made from tough butyl rubber (obtainable from any good garden centre or specialist aquatic supplier). You will also need some old blankets, carpet or newspapers to use as underlay to prevent stones and other sharp objects tearing the lining. Finally, you'll need a sharp knife or scissors, a spirit level to check the edges, some stones or lumps of turf to hold down the edge of the lining, and plenty of sand to cover the lining once it has been installed.

The process of making a pond is as follows:

1. Starting in the centre, begin digging your hole. Dig at least 15 cm (6 inches) deeper than the planned depth, so that you can fit in the underlay and lining.
2. Vary the depth of the hole, so that you will be able to have shallow and deep areas. For example, you may want a hole 30 cm deep at the sides to 80 cm deep in the middle, creating a pond ranging in depth from 15 cm to 65 cm (about 6 inches to just over 2 feet).
3. Once you have dug the hole to more or less the required size, rake over the earth, remove sharp objects such as stones and rocks, and add a thin layer of sand.
4. Lay a blanket (or piece of carpet or newspapers) over the sand.
5. Carefully lay the pond liner on top, keeping it smooth but avoiding overstretching it. Give it an overlap of 10–20 cm at the edges, and then secure it with bricks, stones or pieces of turf.

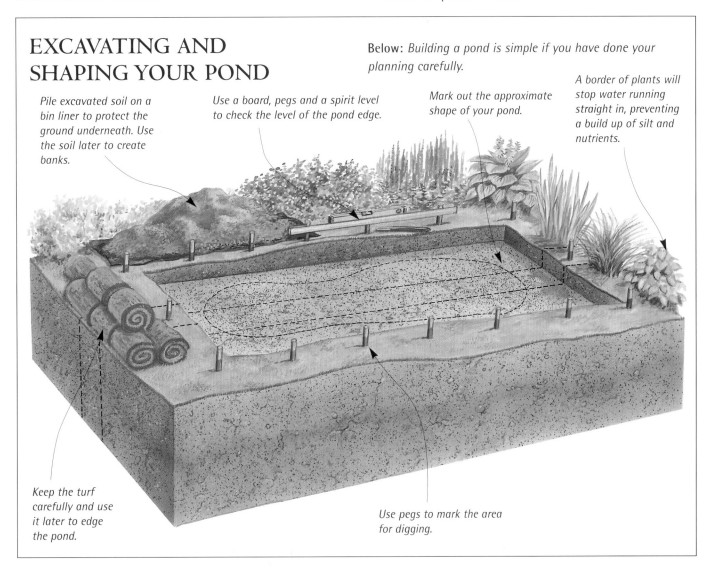

EXCAVATING AND SHAPING YOUR POND

Below: *Building a pond is simple if you have done your planning carefully.*

Pile excavated soil on a bin liner to protect the ground underneath. Use the soil later to create banks.

Use a board, pegs and a spirit level to check the level of the pond edge.

Mark out the approximate shape of your pond.

A border of plants will stop water running straight in, preventing a build up of silt and nutrients.

Keep the turf carefully and use it later to edge the pond.

Use pegs to mark the area for digging.

6. Add a second layer of sand or subsoil (about 10 cm thick) over the lining itself.

7. Fill the pond gradually, to avoid disturbing the soil at the bottom, with a garden hose. Watch out for movement of the lining. As the pond fills up with water, gently release the lining by moving the stones or turf, but make sure the edges are still secure. The liner should eventually exactly fit the contours of the excavation. If you can, it is even better to fill your pond with rainwater, perhaps from a water butt.

8. As a final kick-start to your pond, get a bucketful of water from a neighbour's pond. The tiny creatures and plant life it contains will give a real boost to your pond, accelerating its colonization by other wildlife.

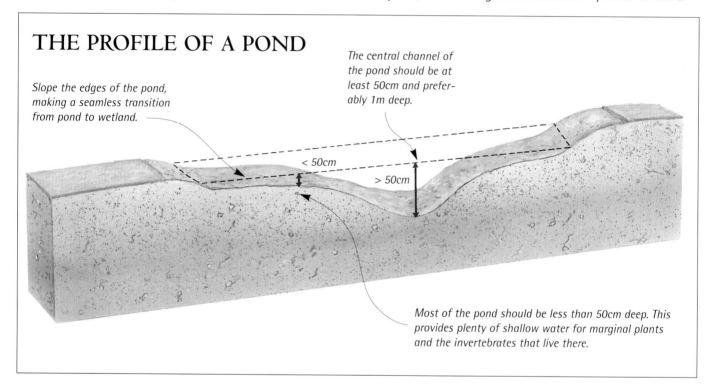

THE PROFILE OF A POND

The central channel of the pond should be at least 50cm and preferably 1m deep.

Slope the edges of the pond, making a seamless transition from pond to wetland.

< 50cm

> 50cm

Most of the pond should be less than 50cm deep. This provides plenty of shallow water for marginal plants and the invertebrates that live there.

Above: *Most of the pond should be shallow with a deeper central area. The deeper water provides a refuge when the pond freezes over in winter.*

Left: *A good selection of (preferably native) aquatic plants will make your pond good for all sorts of wildlife as well as birds – and make it look good too! Choose a selection of submerged, emergent and floating plants (see page 25).*

Stocking your pond with plants

Once your pond is up and running, you will need to stock it with aquatic plants. Ideally, however, you should wait until early spring before you do so.

Plants come in three main types: submerged, floating or emergent, and 'edge'.

- **Submerged:** these provide a regular supply of oxygen into the water, preventing stagnation and the build-up of algae. Good plants include Water-milfoil and Curled Pondweed. Make sure that you avoid the introduced Canadian Pondweed, which will take over.
- **Floating or emergent:** plants such as White and Yellow Water-lily, Amphibious Bistort and Ivy-leaved Duckweed float on the surface; while Yellow Iris and Water Mint stick out of the water and create a beautiful flowering display.
- **Edge plants:** plant Purple Loosestrife, Reedmace and Flowering Rush around the margins, where they will attract insects and other little creatures, and provide a safe haven for amphibians such as frogs and newts.

As always, the best plants are native varieties. Do not, however, take these from the wild, as this is not only anti-social, but also illegal. Most large garden centres and specialist aquatic suppliers now stock a good range of these plants and will advise you on what is best for your pond.

WHERE TO PLANT IN YOUR POND

Below: *Stock your pond with native plants, and include a selection of submerged, floating-leaved, emergent and edge plants to provide a variety of habitats.*

Submerged plants are the oxygenators and need to be planted first, e.g. Rigid Hornwort, Spiked Water-milfoil, Common Water-starwort, Willowmoss.

Floating-leaved plants are perennial favourites, e.g. Broad-leaved Pondweed, White Water-lily, Yellow Water-lily, Water-soldier.

Mix up tall and low-growing emergent plants, e.g. Arrowhead, Brooklime, Mare's Tail, Water Forget-me-not.

Edge plants: The most species rich parts of the pond, e.g. Yellow Iris, Water Plantain.

Above left: *White Water-lilies are not only very attractive, but they also provide food for plenty of insects. In turn, this should attract a range of insect-eating birds to feed in your garden. Don't be too enthusiastic though – water-lilies spread quite quickly and too many can completely cover the surface of your pond, cutting off sunlight to the plants below.*

Above right: *Purple Loosestrife is one of the most attractive native wildflowers to plant in your garden. It thrives at the water's edge and flowers from June to August, with purple-pink blooms on long stalks. It prefers to grow in the sun or semi-shade, and needs damp soil. It attracts insects to its flowers and birds to feed on its seeds.*

Left: *Water-milfoil is just one of many varieties of aquatic plant suitable for your garden pond. To get expert advice on this and other plants visit your local aquatic plant specialist or a reputable garden centre. Never take plants from the wild, as this is illegal.*

Ideally, it is best not to put exotic fish in a pond designed for wildlife, as they often feed on the smaller water creatures and will end up dominating the mini-ecosystem that you have created. A few minnows or stickleback won't do any harm, though, and may even attract a passing Kingfisher.

Other wildlife attracted by the presence of a new pond will include dragonflies and damselflies, which can be almost as varied and fascinating as the birds themselves. Both lay their small eggs into water plants, debris, mud or directly into the water. Having a well-established pond in your garden with all these elements will go a long way to ensuring you see these beauties. Another tip is to have tall emergent plants, such as bulrushes, for the adults to perch on while mating or hunting their prey.

A pond may also attract foxes and even badgers, and of course a range of reptiles and amphibians including Grass Snake, Slow-worm, frogs, toads and newts.

Pond maintenance and safety

Once your pond is up and running, you will need to maintain it. This tends to be harder work at certain times of the year: in autumn, when you will need to clear out fallen leaves on an almost daily basis; in summer, when you will need to clear algae; and in winter, when you must ensure that part of the pond stays ice-free (either by placing a ball in the pond, or by placing a hot object such as a container of boiling water on the ice).

Also bear in mind the safety factor. Garden ponds, even if only a few centimetres deep, can be a danger to young children. If you have children under four years old, or they visit your garden, it is best not to have a pond at all; or if you do have one, make sure that children cannot get access. If you have young children and move into a house that already has a garden pond, consider turning it into a 'marsh': lowering the water level so that only a muddy area remains, then planting appropriate bog-loving plants.

Above: *In the autumn, your pond surface may get covered with fallen leaves, especially if you have large mature trees in your garden. Ideally, try to keep the surface as clear as possible to prevent stagnation and a build up of rotting leaves.*

Below: *During harsh winter weather, make sure you keep at least part of the surface of your pond ice-free. The easiest method is to use a saucepan full of hot water.*

Nesting and Nestboxes

As well as supplying plenty of food and water, you can help birds and bird populations in a very important way by providing places for them to nest and raise their young. This is especially important for species that normally nest in woodland, but have adapted to gardens, where they can find a safe place to breed. Species such as tits, thrushes and Robins can all be encouraged to breed in gardens, either by planting suitable bushes and shrubs (see page 32), or by putting up appropriate nestboxes.

Nestboxes

For birds such as Blue and Great Tits, which normally nest in holes in trees, nestboxes can be a vital lifeline. But it's not just the usual species that use nestboxes: all kinds of birds, from House Martins to Treecreepers and Kestrels to Tawny Owls, can be persuaded that an artificial home is at least as good as a natural one.

Nestboxes are normally made from wood, but other materials can also be used, including composite designs that are supposed to last longer than standard ones. The design is fairly simple: four sides, a bottom, a sloping roof

Below: *A hungry brood of Blue Tits needs a constant supply of food from its busy parents: mainly caterpillars. In spring, it is essential to provide food in your garden for the adults to replenish their own energy resources.*

with an overhang to stop the rain getting in, and most important of all, either a hole or an open front to allow the birds to enter.

Hole-nesting birds include Blue, Great, Coal, Marsh and Willow Tits, Starling, Jackdaw, House Sparrow and Tree Sparrow. Birds that prefer an open-fronted design include Robin, Pied Wagtail and Spotted Flycatcher. Larger boxes are suitable for Barn and Tawny Owls and Kestrel. Other specialist boxes include ones designed especially for Treecreepers and for House Martins, valuable where old trees with loose bark or mud are in short supply.

A standard wooden 'tit-box' should cost no more than £10 or so, although those made from special materials, or designed for larger birds, may cost between £15 and £30. As with all garden bird equipment, it is best to buy a nest-box from a reputable commercial supplier (most do mail order), the RSPB or The Wildlife Trusts.

Ideally, you should put up a nestbox in autumn or winter, which will give the birds a chance to get used to it. Even if spring is already here, it is, however, still worth putting it up and hoping for the best.

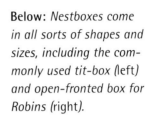

Right: *Nestboxes are not just for commoner garden birds such as tits and sparrows: even specialized species such as the Treecreeper will take to boxes if they are specially designed for them.*

Below: *Nestboxes come in all sorts of shapes and sizes, including the commonly used tit-box (left) and open-fronted box for Robins (right).*

MAKING A NESTBOX

With prices as low as under £10, it is only really worth making nestboxes if you are going to do so in bulk, either for your own garden or to share with others. You really don't need to have advanced do-it-yourself skills, just some suitable equipment and tools:

- Planks of wood measuring around 1-2 metres (just over 3-6 feet) long, about 15 cm (6 inches) wide, and about 15–20 mm (0.6–0.8 inches) thick.
- Small nails or panel pins.
- A good quality wood saw.
- Something to make a hinge for the lid: ideally a strip of rubber taken from an old tyre.
- A hook and eye to secure the lid so that predators can't get in, but you can.
- A drill with the right-sized bit to make the circular entrance hole.
- A tape measure.

Once you have everything you need, the process is fairly straightforward. Bear in mind that all measurements (apart from the size of the entrance hole) are fairly rough-and-ready: precision really isn't that important.

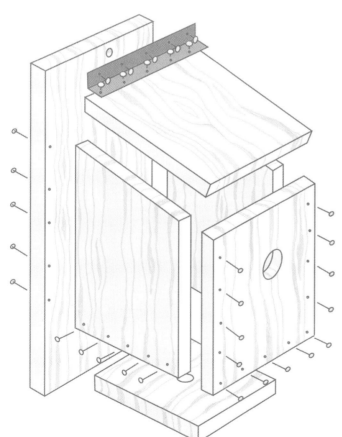

1. Mark out the plank(s) with the dimensions required. The side panels should be approximately 170-180 mm (6.5-7 inches) long; the top 170 mm (6.5 inches) long; and the base panel 150 mm (6 inches) square. Make sure that the back panel has a minimum length of 250 mm (10 inches).
2. Cut the wood into six pieces. Make all the cuts except one at right angles; but, for the two side panels, cut at a shallow angle so that the roof will slope.
3. Nail the two side panels to the base, leaving space above and below for fixing the back panel to a tree or fence post when the box is finished.
4. Drill a small hole or holes in the base to allow for drainage and ventilation. Then nail the base onto the two side panels and back panel.
5. Drill a hole in the front panel, roughly three quarters of the way up. This should be about 25–28 mm (1–1.1 inches) in diameter for tits, and 32 mm (1.25 inches) in diameter for House and Tree Sparrows.
6. Nail the front panel onto the nestbox.
7. Put on the roof, using a strip of rubber as a hinge. The front should overhang by 20 mm (0.75 inches) or so to keep out rain. Secure the roof using a hook and eye so that you can make regular inspections and open the box easily for cleaning.
8. Drill a small hole in the tops and bottom of the back panel for fixing to a tree, post or fence.
9. Finally, treat the outside surfaces of the box with a wood-preserving agent such as creosote, or a branded preserver. Do not treat the inside of the box, as it may harm the birds.

Left and right: *Making your own nestbox may seem like hard work, but in fact it's not too difficult or time-consuming, especially if you are making a few at a time. Just make sure you follow the instructions carefully!*

Siting a nestbox

Having put so much care and attention into the making of your nestbox, or money into buying it, don't throw it all away by putting it in the wrong place.

You should choose the site for a nestbox carefully. Ideally, it should be at a reasonable height (at least 1.5 metres (5 feet) above the ground; and facing anywhere between northwest and southeast. Facing your box in a southerly or westerly direction may run the risk of overheating the eggs and chicks, unless it is protected by shade.

Make sure that you affix your nestbox carefully, as strong winds can easily dislodge it. Use strong nails or preferably wood screws; or, if attaching it to a living tree, fix it using wire, to avoid damage to the trunk or branch.

Nestboxes are an easy target for predators, including squirrels, cats and even woodpeckers. There isn't really a lot that you can do about this, but at least keep it away from obvious points at which a predator could gain access.

Finally, be careful! Climbing up ladders to put up nestboxes can be dangerous, so have someone to help you.

Maintaining a nestbox

Once up, a nestbox doesn't need much looking after: just make sure that you clear out the debris after the breeding season is over, and give the inside of the box a good clean to remove any lingering parasites and dirt. Otherwise, the best thing to do with nestboxes is to leave them alone: resist the temptation to peek inside at frequent intervals, as it will disturb the nesting birds and runs the risk of attracting the attention of predators.

If you want to find out more, the BTO has produced an excellent practical guide: *Nestboxes*, by Chris du Feu. This can be obtained direct from the BTO, which also organizes National Nestbox Week every February. For further details, contact the BTO (see *Useful Addresses* for details).

Above: *Some surprising species will breed in garden nestboxes, including the Spotted Flycatcher, which prefers an openfronted design. Watch them fly off, catch an insect in mid-air, and return to the nestbox to feed their young.*

Below: *When siting your nestbox, ensure you position it at least 1.5 metres above the ground, facing away from the glare of the midday sun. This nestbox is suitable for tits.*

Above: *You can make your garden better for nesting birds by planting a wide variety of shrubs and bushes with dense foliage, preferably native varieties, where the birds can be safe and secure from predators.*

Left: *More than any other common garden bird, Robins nest in an amazing range of bizarre places. In the past, these have included inside watering cans, under the bonnet of vehicles and, in this case, at the back of a tool cupboard!*

Planting for nesting birds

As well as providing artificial nestboxes, you can help birds in your garden by planting suitable shrubs and trees in which they can build their nest. Almost anything with dense foliage is suitable: even the dreaded *leylandii* cypresses that cause so many disputes between neighbours. More aesthetically pleasing plants include climbers such as clematis, ivy and honeysuckle; hedgerow plants such as holly, hawthorn and privet; bushes and shrubs such as elder and bramble; or even trees such as oak and beech. Most of these also provide a bonus in the shape of insect food, fruit or berries. For further details see the *Plants to Attract Birds* section on page 140.

Shelter and Safety

Attracting birds to visit your garden is all well and good, but what if you expose them to danger? Disease and predators are both very real threats, and making sure that your garden provides a safe haven for the birds is just as important as providing food and water in the first place.

In *Troubleshooting* (see pages 94–9) I will cover the major pests and predators such as rats and mice, squirrels, Magpies, Sparrowhawks and of course cats. In the meantime, there is one major thing that you can do to help make your garden a safer place for all the wild creatures that visit it: practice good hygiene.

Hygiene

Good hygiene is basically common sense. As I have already said, you need to keep a close eye on your birdtable, feeders and birdbath, making sure that they are as clean as possible. You can do this by sweeping away old food with a soft brush (preferably into a dustbin via dustpan) and giving all exposed surfaces a regular scrub with a stiff brush and some soap and water.

Never use chemical cleaners on surfaces, as traces may remain and can easily poison birds via the food that they eat. Small birds are especially vulnerable, as their very light body weight (sometimes only a few grams) means that it doesn't take much to poison them.

Once you have given your birdfeeders a really good clean, make sure all surfaces (inside and out) are dry before you put them back: dampness will only accelerate the process of decay when you fill them with food. Likewise, always rinse birdbaths thoroughly with clean water, so that no traces of soap remain.

Disease

Very occasionally, you may have a bigger problem: that of an outbreak of disease at your bird-feeding station. This particularly affects birds that feed in flocks such as tits, sparrows, finches and Starlings. Keep an eye out for birds that appear listless, or whose plumage looks more tatty than is usual.

The problem will probably soon clear itself up, but, if the symptoms persist, and especially if you find an abnormal quantity of dead or dying birds in your garden, then notify the RSPB at once.

Below: *Keep your birdfeeders, birdtable and birdbath clean to prevent disease, but don't use chemical cleaners as these may poison the very birds you are trying to attract. This Tree Sparrow is a fairly uncommon garden visitor.*

Gardens for Birds

Different gardens suit different birds, as you might expect. A large, mature garden in a rural setting is likely to attract a greater variety of species than would a small patch of land in the centre of a city, though a well-stocked garden in a suburb, near a park or an area of water, may attract more than either.

People's time, money and inclination vary too, so in this chapter I offer three options, depending on what you want to achieve:
- The Basic Bird Garden.
- Moving On.
- The Advanced Bird Garden.

Feel free to mix and match from these, or ignore some of the suggestions: they are not recipes, but ways of getting you to think about what you can realistically achieve for birds in your garden.

The Basic Bird Garden

Many people think that, because their garden is too small, or too urban, or doesn't have enough plants, they will not be able to attract birds to it. Nothing could be farther from the truth: any garden, no matter how unprepossessing it may seem, can be transformed into a haven for at least some of your local birds.

Another argument that people put forward for doing nothing is the time involved. They pick up a book like this, see instructions for making a nestbox or creating a garden pond, and assume that, to make a difference, they will have to spend every waking hour digging, hammering and nailing things together.

Finally, there is the cost. Flick through the RSPB catalogue and you will see feeders of every shape and size,

Left: *Even if you have a small garden only, you can make it a real haven for birds by creating a series of 'mini-habitats' in which they can shelter, roost, feed and nest.*

Above top and above: *A suburban bird garden, especially one with nearby parkland or woods, is the perfect place for Wood Pigeons to feed and nest.*

Above: *A sturdy, well-made birdtable will suit any garden and is a quick and easy way to provide a range of food to attract a variety of different species. Birdtables cost between £20 and £80, depending on the design.*

one of them, as you have either bought, borrowed, or been given this book. Nevertheless, I shall assume that you are busy, poor and lazy, or – to put it more politely – that you have a job or other occupation that consumes much of your time, a family or hobby that consumes most of your money, and a relatively small garden which doesn't look all that promising for birds. Having read this section, you will, I hope, decide that making your garden more bird-friendly will take only the minimum of time, effort and expense, and that the rewards, for you and for the birds, will be well worth it.

The £100-a-year, 30-minutes-a-week bird garden

Can you afford two quid, and half an hour of your time, a week? If so, read on. This section will tell you what you need to do, how much it will cost, and how long it will take.

Let's start with the cost. Much of the initial investment is up front, but nevertheless should average at around £2 per week over the whole year. Capital investment means that, over a long period, it will work out even cheaper. The money is spent as follows:

- £20 on a basic birdtable.
- £15 for two feeders: one for peanuts, the other for seeds.
- £10 on a nestbox.
- £10 on a basic birdbath.
- £15 on a large bag of sunflower hearts.
- £15 on a large bag of mixed seed for the birdtable.
- £15 on a large bag of peanuts.

costing anything up to £100, and designed to hold gourmet foods costing more per kilo than the stuff that you give to your kids. You do a back-of-an-envelope calculation and work out that, by feeding the birds, you will soon find that your home has been repossessed and that your family is out on the street.

As a result, many people do absolutely nothing to attract birds to their garden. Fortunately, you can't be

With this, you are providing all the basic essentials: a range of food for different species at different levels; a place to bathe and to drink; and a place where one lucky pair of birds can build a nest and raise its young. Okay, so you may have to supplement the feeding with kitchen scraps and leftovers to make it last the whole year, but you really will be providing a perfectly acceptable service station for the birds in your area. And I haven't cheated on the prices: these products are all available at this cost from major birdfood manufacturers.

As for time, well, even half an hour is probably more than you will need. All you need to do is to refill your feeders regularly, clear away any uneaten or mouldy food, and top up the water in your birdbath, say twice a week. Add in a couple of hours, say every three months, to take down and clean all the equipment, and that is all the time that you need to spare. So, no excuses accepted!

If you can spare more time, you can always turn your hand to making birdtables and nestboxes for yourself, though to be honest this is fairly uneconomic unless you are planning to do it in bulk. You could always try getting together with a couple of friends and each making a specific piece of equipment for each of your gardens.

Right: *Nestboxes are just perfect substitutes for holes in trees and will attract species that evolved to live in woodland, such as this Great Tit. Given a good supply of food this hungry brood should all manage to fledge successfully in a couple of weeks.*

Below: *A good bird-friendly garden should have a range of places for birds to feed, nest, drink and bathe. Experiment with moving things around until you are sure you have found the ideal places for them.*

Providing food, water and a place to nest is only the beginning. You should also take a look at your garden design, and the kinds of plants that you have there. If you have just moved in, then spend a few months watching the changes in the garden, and which birds are attracted to which particular plants. You may find

Left: *The Collared Dove arrived in Britain fifty years ago only, having spread rapidly across Continental Europe. Today it is a very familiar garden visitor, especially in suburban and rural areas.*

Below: *Native shrubs such as this Rowan provide a welcome supply of juicy red berries in autumn and early winter: ideal for insect-eating birds such as thrushes, Robins and even Waxwings to gorge themselves on.*

that a particular plant may not be much in favour for part of the year, but that once it produces seeds or berries the birds love it.

Creating a garden pond is beyond the scope of this low budget, low maintenance garden, but allowing a corner of your garden to 'go wild' takes little time or expense. Just let nature take its course – and don't cut back the brambles, ivy or nettles at the bottom of the garden, which are all homes for invertebrates, thus providing food for the birds.

If you are sticking to the £100 limit, you may want to cut down on some of the equipment (say the nestbox and one of the feeders), make substitutions (e.g. use a kitchen bowl as a temporary birdbath), or do a bit of DIY and make your own birdtable or nestbox. That way, you will have more money to spend on plants. Alternatively, try to beg or borrow cuttings from a friend or neighbour, or ask for garden-centre gift vouchers for birthday, Christmas, father's day, or mother's day presents.

The birds that come into your garden will, of course, depend on where you live. You can be pretty sure, however, that, by providing the mini service station detailed above, you will attract a good range of the commoner species in your area. Species such as tits, House Sparrows and Greenfinches are becoming more and more dependent on food provided by us; while Robins, Dunnocks and Collared Doves are close behind. Any one of these is a delight to watch; so, even if your effort attracts only a few more birds, it will have been worthwhile.

Below: *Jays are regular visitors to gardens, where they prey on songbirds' nests and eggs in spring and summer, and feed on acorns in autumn and winter. During the autumn, there is often an influx of Jays from Europe into eastern and southern Britain.*

Moving On

Once you have put up a couple of birdfeeders, a table and a nestbox, it's easy to sit back and simply enjoy the show. However, after a while, you may begin to feel a bit dissatisfied; after all, nobody wants to watch repeats all the time.

The problem is, if you only have a limited range of feeders and food, that you will attract only the same clients. Just as a café or restaurant needs to vary its decor and menu to attract new clients and keep old ones, so you need to consider making some additions and changes to your bird service station.

I've put together an 'upgrade', where, by spending an extra couple of hundred pounds a year, and a bit more time and effort, you can really make a difference to your garden birds. The extra money is spent as follows:

- £50-£75 on a more advanced and larger birdtable, with a removable roof to allow open access in fine weather.
- £20-£25 on a metal, squirrel-proof 'cage' feeder to enable small birds such as tits to feed while keeping squirrels out.
- £40-£50 on three large metal feeders (two for seeds, one for peanuts), to be strategically placed around your garden to attract 'passing trade'.

Above: *Spending a bit more effort, time and money allows you to provide a wider range of different feeders containing a variety of foods, each specially designed to attract particular species.*

- £10-£15 on a supply of fat-rich 'cakes', to attract a wider range of species, including Blackcap and Great Spotted Woodpecker.
- £10-£20 on a supply of mealworms for species such as Robins and Jays.
- £20 on a couple of extra nestboxes, one with the usual hole and the other open-fronted for Robins.
- £20-£30 on a larger and sturdier birdbath.
- Any remaining cash you can afford on extra food to stock up those feeders.

Give away your old, unwanted equipment to friends: with any luck, they will get the bird-feeding bug as well.

By increasing the number of feeding points, and varying the food more widely (especially with mealworms and fat bars), you should begin to attract less-usual species to your garden. Although, again, the range and make-up of species depends on the size and location of your garden, you should manage to increase the number of species feeding there by at least 50 per cent.

Biodiversity

A more long-term method of increasing diversity of species visiting your garden is to increase its general biodiversity. This is not as difficult as it sounds: there are various relatively simple ways in which you can increase biodiversity in your garden.

Create a garden pond: nothing will change your garden so much as adding a permanent water feature. Ponds attract all kinds of other wildlife, notably a wide range of insects and other invertebrates, which provide an alternative, natural source of food for your garden birds. Ponds also provide excellent places for birds to drink and bathe, so long as you design them with at least one shallow, sloping edge so that the birds are able to gain access to the water easily.

Let part of your garden go wild: if you have limited space, you may feel that you simply can't afford the luxury of sharing it with the wildlife. However, you really don't need to do very much in order to make your garden more wildlife-friendly: even a small pile of logs in one corner, or letting part of your lawn grow a little longer, will enable small creatures to find a home.

Right: *The* pièce de résistance *of a wildlife garden is surely a well-designed garden pond: it may take hard work, but it will be worth it!*

Plant large, native shrubs and trees: plants such as Honeysuckle and Elder produce flowers to attract insects during the spring and summer, and luscious ripe berries for the birds to feed on in the autumn. They also look great for most of the year!

Change your flower-beds: changing the balance of your garden, from foreign, exotic plants to a few native ones can make a big difference to the birds. Native plants, such as Primrose and Red Campion, attract many insects, including butterflies and their caterpillars, all of which will attract more birds in late summer. Even non-native varieties such as Buddleia are excellent for butterflies; while many plants produce seeds, which will attract finches in late summer and autumn.

Plant climbers: climbing plants such as Ivy and Clematis are brilliant for birds, as once they have grown they provide the perfect secluded place to build a nest. Species such as Robin and Blackbird will take advantage of most climbing plants.

Left: *Elder flowers attract insects during the spring and summer, which in turn attract a variety of birds. In the autumn, the Elder's berries are also most appealing to birds.*

Below: *Old Man's Beard is a well known climbing plant, although not often seen in gardens. It provides perfect nesting sites – why not plant one in your garden?*

The Advanced Bird Garden

If you really want to turn your garden into a five-star hotel for the birds, then the sky's the limit. You can spend hundreds of pounds, and many hours of your time. Indeed, looking after the birds in your garden can become not so much a hobby, but more a way of life.

Obviously, as well as being able to devote this much time, money and effort to making your garden attractive to birds, you require a fairly large, mature garden in the first place. It also needs to be in the right location: there's no point putting in this much into your garden if it is in the middle of a birdless zone. Not that you necessarily have to live in a rural location. Modern farming practices have rendered much of the countryside, especially in eastern England, pretty devoid of birds, whereas towns, villages and even some city centres can harbour a wide range of species. The urban oasis is a relatively new concept, but a very important one.

Before you embark on an ambitious programme of turning over your garden to the birds, ask yourself a few pertinent questions:

- Can I really afford the time and money that will be required to carry this out?
- Is my family behind me on this? The garden should never be seen as purely a bird reserve: it is for you and your family and friends to enjoy too. If this means making a few compromises, then so be it.
- Will I enjoy the process of creating a bird-friendly garden as much as the end result? Some people have a passion for DIY, and enjoy the physical work of gardening as much as sitting back and enjoying the fruits of their labours. Others take the opposite view: that the hard work is merely a means to an end. I only ask, because you will need to take a fairly early view as to whether you want to do the work yourself, or get help from professional gardeners. You may also prefer to buy your feeding equipment rather than making it; that's up to you.

So what can you do, and how much will it cost? Well, in some ways, the cost is also up to you. Look through a catalogue of bird-feeding equipment and you will see everything from a simple peanut feeder costing under £5, to a futuristic mega-feeder retailing at around £100.

Above: *If you are lucky enough to have Swallows nesting in your garden, you will be able to enjoy the comings and goings of the parent birds as they feed their hungry young.*

Below: *Like many small birds, House Sparrows love to give their feathers a good clean-up using a birdbath. Make sure you keep the water clean by changing it regularly.*

Left: *If you live in the countryside and have a large garden with mature trees you are likely to attract all kinds of visitors from surrounding habitats.*

Above: *Although an ornamental, non-native species, Pyracantha is not only attractive but provides a rich source of berries, attracting pigeons and thrushes.*

Each of these does its job perfectly well: it really is up to you what combination of food and feeders you buy.

Food and feeders

I would say, however, that the key to creating a truly bird-friendly garden is a combination of both natural food-stuffs and those provided by human beings. Choice is the key: each species prefers to feed on a specific range of foods, delivered in a fairly specific manner.

A good combination of food and feeders would be:

- A number of peanut feeders, placed on poles, hanging from tree branches, or stuck on the outside of your kitchen window so that you can get close-up views.
- An even larger number of seed feeders, also placed in a variety of different locations and contexts to allow different birds to feed.

- A large birdtable, preferably with a roof (allowing easy access for cleaning and that can be removed during fine weather to give the birds more room to feed). There are a wide variety of designs available from garden centres, commercial suppliers and so on.
- At least one birdbath – preferably two, of different sizes and depths, to allow different-sized birds to drink and bathe.
- Several 'fat bars' or 'cakes', which tend to attract species that do not normally come to feeders such as wintering Blackcaps.
- At least one squirrel-proof feeder if you have squirrels in your garden (and who doesn't?).
- A dish or two of mealworms to attract those bird species that prefer live food rather than nuts or seeds, such as Jays, Robins and Dunnocks.

45

Above: *Nestboxes aren't just for small birds: even species such as the Tawny Owl can be attracted to breed in them.*

Below: *A shortage of mud in your local area may mean that House Martins are unable to build their own nests (left). So why not give them a helping hand by putting up specially-designed artificial nestboxes (right)?*

You should also try to plant as many natural sources of food as possible, including:

- Native wildflowers for their nectar and seeds, and to attract butterflies, moths and other insects.
- Berry-bearing plants, such as elder, hawthorn and bramble, which provide juicy and nutritious fruit in the autumn and winter.
- Trees, such as apple and plum, to provide fruit and to attract insects.

Nesting birds

Regarding nesting birds, the most important thing is to have a range of plants in your garden, especially trees, bushes and climbing plants that attract roosting birds and provide places for them to nest. In the short term, offering a range of nestboxes is also a good idea. I would suggest the following as a start:

- Two or three 'classic' tit boxes with an entrance hole, for Blue and Great Tits, and if you still have them in your neighbourhood, House Sparrows.
- At least one larger box with an entrance hole of at least 45 mm, for Starlings.
- One or two open-fronted boxes, for Robins, and Spotted Flycatchers if you have them in your garden.

If you are more ambitious, you may also try some specialized nestboxes, which you can either make yourself or buy ready-made. Some tried-and-tested designs include:

- Wedge-shaped box for Treecreepers.
- Large open box for Kestrels or Barn Owls.
- Nesting tube for Tawny Owls.
- Cup-shaped 'boxes' for Swallows and House Martins.
- Communal nestbox designed to attract several pairs of House Sparrows to breed together.

Biodiversity

Finally, you could make more major changes to your garden layout in order to increase biodiversity and thereby to attract more birds. If you choose to go down this route, I would recommend investing in one of the 'wildlife garden makeover' books recommended in *Further Reading*. A relatively recent book on the subject is *Chris Packham's Back Garden Nature Reserve*. Chris takes an entertaining and practical attitude to wildlife gardening: never forgetting that you share your garden with the wildlife, and that wildlife gardening should always be fun.

Chris Packham recommends:

- If you don't have one already, **create a garden pond**. Sure, it will take time, effort and a bit of money, but it will transform your garden, not just for birds, but also for all kinds of other wildlife.
- Turn over at least part of your lawn to a **wildflower meadow**: planting native meadow flowers that will in turn attract plenty of insects for the birds to feed on.
- Let part of your garden become a **wilderness,** allowing stinging nettles, brambles and other 'weeds' to take over, to create a more natural habitat.
- Stop using garden pesticides and herbicides, and instead use natural remedies such as nematode worms to control pests. Also by encouraging plenty of wildlife you will soon achieve natural pest control!

These changes may not seem huge, but – believe me – they will make a great difference to the biodiversity of your garden, and that means more birds for you to enjoy.

Below: *If you are a really keen wildlife gardener, why not give over part of your lawn to planting a wildflower meadow, to attract insects and provide seeds for birds?*

Above: *Kestrels are another bird of prey that take readily to artificial boxes, preferring a wide, deep box with an open front. This female is incubating her clutch of four or five eggs.*

Understanding Garden Bird Behaviour

This chapter will help you to understand some of the common and more unusual behaviour of garden birds. I hope that it will spur you on to watch them more closely, and to learn as much as you can about the lifecycle of some of our most common – yet most fascinating – birds. It covers the study of bird behaviour, including feeding, drinking, bathing, breeding, nesting, moulting, and flocking.

Studying Bird Behaviour

The study of animal behaviour or, as it is more properly known, ethology, is a relatively young science. Only during the twentieth century did students of birds emerge from the museum and laboratory and get out in the field to look at them. Men such as Sir Julian Huxley, Konrad Lorenz and Niko Tinbergen were pioneers, spending long hours simply watching birds and recording their day-to-day habits and behaviour. They discovered some amazing things about even our most common birds, and later applied this to animal behaviour in general, developing some of the most important theories of modern science.

You might think that everything that there is to know about birds has now been learned, but in fact that is far from the case. Only a few years ago, scientists still thought most birds were basically faithful to their partner, and that if infidelity did occur it was inevitably on the part of the male. Nowadays, in part thanks to the study of common birds

Left: *Starlings gather together in huge numbers at dusk, especially in winter, and may be seen flying in large flocks over your garden.*

Above and right: *The Rose-ringed (or Ring-necked) Parakeet is a newcomer to many gardens in the London suburbs, where it appears to thrive. Chiffchaffs are common in most gardens.*

such as the Dunnock, we now realise that the battle of the sexes is a constant one, and that, if anything, females can be even more fickle than are their long-suffering partners.

New kinds of behaviour are being reported all the time, especially as new designs of feeders and more varieties of food are bringing more and more new species into our gardens. The recent change in the overwintering and migratory habits of two of our commonest warblers, Blackcap and Chiffchaff, were observed partly in gardens, while the effects on our native species of new arrivals such as the exotic-looking Rose-ringed Parakeet may also be observed from our kitchen windows.

Even if you don't make a momentous discovery, you will still enjoy watching your garden birds more closely, and making notes about the behaviours you observe. So, make a resolution to record what you see, and, if you're not sure why a bird is behaving in a particular way, don't be afraid to ask someone: it may prove to be more unusual than you think.

Above: *Juvenile birds such as this Blackcap are especially vulnerable to predators, so often hide deep in foliage, among the branches of trees and shrubs.*

Your garden can be a microcosm of what is happening on a wider scale, and reflects the changes happening elsewhere. The great advantage is that, unlike a place that you have to visit, you are likely to be observing your garden on a regular basis anyway, perhaps while doing the cooking or washing-up, or when relaxing in a sitting-room or conservatory. You are likely to put in more hours observing from home than anywhere else, which gives you a better chance of noting unusual behaviour, and also more of an opportunity to understand what is normal.

Left: *Pheasants are attractive birds, which display a wide range of behaviour. This male is calling from a prominent perch to defend his territory against rival males.*

Seasons and behaviour

Bird behaviour is intimately linked with two factors: the seasons and the weather. The seasons dictate when a bird forms feeding flocks, chooses a mate and begins courtship, defends a territory, or begins to moult; while sudden changes in the weather, especially severe cold or drought, also has a profound effect on the habits of birds.

Changes in day-length (i.e. the relative amount of light and darkness) affect birds by acting on their internal nervous system. So, in early spring, longer hours of daylight are the trigger for the start of courtship and nesting activity; and, once the breeding season is over, in autumn, shorter daylight hours are what drive migrants such as warblers, swallows and martins to migrate south.

The weather has more short-term, but much more rapid and acute, effects on birds in your garden. A sudden cold snap, especially when it is accompanied by snowfall, spells disaster for small songbirds, which have to eat constantly in order to survive the winter. A few hours without food often leads to rapid deterioration and eventual death. In summer, a long spell of very sunny weather, although at first good for breeding birds, can cause problems through drought leading to a different kind of food shortage. On the other hand, prolonged rain is also bad for breeding birds, as it may chill eggs and young birds.

Obviously, the weather varies from year to year, but over time its effects should even themselves out, so that bird populations recover from a hard winter or long drought. Now that global climate change is upon us, however, we may be seeing longer-term shifts in the habits, behaviour and populations of some of our most familiar birds (see page 66).

Birds' seasons are not quite the same as the traditional meanings of spring, summer, autumn and winter. In some ways, these terms can be confusing (such as in books that refer to 'summer' and 'winter' plumages when they really mean 'breeding' and 'non-breeding' ones). I prefer to think of three broad 'seasons', defined by the actual behaviour of the birds rather than strictly by calendar.

Above: *Winter thrushes such as this Redwing and Fieldfare join forces with resident species such as the Blackbird to feed on windfall apples in autumn and winter. Fruit provides an excellent energy resource, especially in hard weather.*

Below: *Severe weather conditions in winter mean it is all the more important to keep your pond or birdbath ice free. This Mistle Thrush has had no luck trying to drink from this pond.*

These are:
- **Breeding**: the period of establishing territory through song, courtship, nest-building, egg-laying and rearing chicks to the point of fledging and/or leaving the nest.
- **Post-breeding**: the fairly short period following the breeding season when adult birds usually moult into a fresh plumage, while young birds are exploring the area around where they were born; and migrants are getting ready to leave.
- **Non-breeding**: the season during which most birds join up with others from their own (and sometimes other) species and form flocks, usually in order to remain safe and maximize their chances of finding food; or when some species are absent from our shores because they prefer to spend the winter elsewhere.

The edges of these categories are inevitably somewhat blurred, not least because each species times its breeding very differently. For example, a few species, such as pigeons and doves, can breed virtually all year around, and birdsong can sometimes be heard as early as January if the weather is mild. Recent mild winters have led to reports of some songbirds beginning to breed in late autumn, because they are confused by the high temperatures.

On the other hand, although some 'summer visitors' (i.e. migrants from Africa) get here in March (e.g. Chiffchaff),

Above: Chaffinches build a cup-shaped nest out of moss and grass, usually in a bush, hedgerow or small tree. The male will sing his characteristic song from a prominent perch nearby.

many others do not arrive back here until late April or even May, with some, such as the Spotted Flycatcher, occasionally arriving in late May. Many migrants spend hardly any time with us, with most Cuckoos and Swifts departing the country by August. Others, such as the House Martin, stay on well into September and even October in some areas.

In addition, there are, of course, many regional differences. You would not expect garden birds in Shetland to begin breeding at the same time as those in Cornwall, and you would be right. Northern Britain may experience a time lag of up to three weeks compared to the south regarding the arrival of summer visitors; and birds will leave northern parts earlier too, to begin their migration southwards to Europe and beyond.

Birds' calendars are far from precise, and many will alter their arrival and departure times depending on the prevailing weather conditions. Meanwhile, global warming is definitely changing patterns of behaviour, so that the distinctions between the traditional seasons are becoming even less clear, with spring arriving earlier, and autumn going on later, than ever before.

Feeding Behaviour

Probably the most common form of behaviour you will regularly observe in your garden is that of feeding. Different species feed on different foods, using different methods, which keeps them ecologically separated from their relatives. For example, the Chaffinch is mainly a ground-feeder, while Goldfinches prefer to sit on seed-heads and use their very sharp beaks to prise out the contents.

By putting up a variety of feeders, you may be blurring the distinctions found in Nature. For example, your peanut or seed feeders will attract several different species of tit and finch, sparrows, Starlings and Robins. These are now thrust into artificial competition with each other, though if you continue to put out food on a regular basis there should be enough to go around.

Some species are more specialized than others are, preferring to stick to a diet of seeds or insects. Others switch depending on the time of year, feeding their young on caterpillars and other insects, while eating seeds or nuts outside the breeding season. Some, such as the Blackcap, have changed their diet in recent years, taking a far wider variety of natural foods (and those provided by us) than before. Some have discovered new foodstuffs relatively recently, such as the celebrated ability of Blue Tits to pierce the foil tops of milk bottles to get at the contents, or wintering Chiffchaffs coming to peanut feeders.

Left: *A few decades ago Blue Tits learned how to drink milk by making holes in the foil bottle-tops. Nowadays, as doorstep milk delivery continues to decline, so does this habit.*

Thirty years or so ago, Siskins were an unusual visitor to gardens, generally only visiting those near large areas of woodland. Today, they are a familiar garden bird for many, and jostle at the feeders with their commoner cousins such as Greenfinches.

So watch out for familiar species taking new foods, or feeding in a new way, and keep a record (see page 65). It may prove to be a one-off, or the start of something big.

Below: *In winter, insect-eaters such as this Blackcap change their diet to suit the changing weather, feeding on energy-rich foods such as Cotoneaster berries.*

Drinking and Bathing

Birds need water to drink and to bathe in, and the ways that they take advantage of a regular supply can provide us with hours of entertainment. Most birds need to drink between once and three or four times a day, largely depending on their diet. For example, a seedeater, such as the Greenfinch, will need to drink more often than a bird that mainly eats insects, such as the Wren, because seeds contain less moisture.

When they do drink, each bird has its own method of doing so. Most are constantly on the lookout for danger, as drinking makes them vulnerable to attack by a cat or other predator. Songbirds have, therefore, adopted the habit of taking several swift sips, often making several quick visits to a bird-bath or pond do so.

The same applies to bathing, which is essential in order to keep feathers clean and in good condition. Most birds bathe by sitting in shallow water and ruffling their feathers rapidly, in order to cover all of their plumage without the risk of its becoming completely waterlogged. Afterwards they will often sit in a sunny place to dry, preening to keep their feathers in good working order.

A few species, including House Sparrows, prefer to 'dust-bathe', using the grit and sand in dust to clean their feathers by abrading them. This has the added advantage of removing many parasites that are immune to being dislodged by water alone.

Above: *Grey Wagtails may visit your garden to drink and bathe, especially if you have a pond that attracts insects for them to feed as well.*

Left: *Watching even a common bird such as a Starling as it bathes gives you a real insight into bird behaviour. Bathing in a birdbath is safer as cats are less likely to reach them.*

Breeding Behaviour

The subject of breeding behaviour is huge. Entire books have been written on just one element such as birdsong, while many hours of scientific observation and theorizing have gone into trying to explain what it going on.

However, don't be daunted by this: anyone can appreciate the beauty of a thrush's song, or enjoy the antics of rival male Robins or a family party of Long-tailed Tits. All you need is a basic understanding of what is going on and what stage in the process you are observing.

Along with feeding, breeding is the most important part of bird behaviour. Only by breeding will a bird pass on its genes to another generation. For many songbirds, this is urgent, since their life expectancy rarely exceeds three or four years.

Breeding behaviour can be divided up into several constituent parts, though inevitably these do overlap, as they are all part of the same process.

Birdsong and calls

Birdsong is one of the great joys for us. Yet it has an importance far exceeding its aesthetic beauty. Male birds sing for two reasons: to maintain their newly acquired territory against the invasion of rival males; and to win a mate amongst the population of available females. They usually sing at two main times: very early morning and late afternoon and evening. The so-called 'dawn chorus' is often almost over by daybreak, as by the time that it gets light the birds have more important things to do such as find food.

Many birds choose a particular place to sing, often a high point of a tree or building, where they are more likely to be heard both by rivals and by females.

To hear the beauty of birdsong, all you need is a pair of ears. Truly to appreciate its complexity, however, you have to slow it down using a tape recorder. Then, you can hear that what appears to be a single note is in fact a complex medley of sounds, seemingly uttered simultaneously, yet each actually distinct.

Above: *The Robin is the only garden bird that sings virtually throughout the year, even in autumn and winter when other birds are relatively quiet.*

Below: *The Chaffinch sings in early spring from a prominent perch on a bush or tree, often in gardens.*

Above: *Collared Doves court much of the year round, taking advantage of mild weather and regular food supplies to raise several broods.*

Below: *Normally a shy bird, spring transforms the male Dunnock into a real show-off, as he defends his territory and tries to attract a mate.*

Recognizing birdsong takes practice, and you may want to use CDs or tapes to learn the different songs and calls. To be honest, however, there is no substitute for experience, and the great thing about your garden birds is that they will be there day after day, enabling you to get used to the different rhythms, tones and pitches that distinguish one songster from the rest.

Another prominent set of calls is those used in alarm: for example the loud call of the Blackbird when a cat is approaching. Learning these may help you spot predators such as Sparrowhawks.

A good way to learn about birdsong is to go along to one of the many local Wildlife Trusts' International Dawn Chorus days, held in May every year; call your local Trust for more details.

Courtship

It used to be thought that birds basically mated for life, and indeed some, such as the Mute Swan, often do. But amongst smaller birds, lax sexual behaviour is commonplace, with all kinds of dubious practices, including promiscuity and partner-swapping.

Right: *Male Robins are aggressive birds, often fighting until one is injured or even killed. They fight in order to defend their territory against an intruder.*

This is, however, all for good reasons. It's not just vital that a bird reproduces, but that it does so with the right partner: to produce strong, healthy young that will in turn survive to breed and reproduce themselves. In addition, a male bird may not know that the chicks it is raising are actually his, since only the mother can be sure. So, by having as many partners as possible, a male bird strengthens his chances of passing on his genes. The female, on the other hand, is looking for a healthy father for her chicks; and if that means having sex with several partners, so be it.

Hence the battles in spring. Males are not just fighting to win a territory once, but need to defend it over and over again against their rivals.

In the meantime, they must court the female, often involving complex and ritualistic behaviour such as pecking, displaying and calling. This is especially noticeable in the humble Feral Pigeon, whose males turn into positive Romeos as they attempt to woo the apparently uninterested female.

Even after the pair is together, the male will devote much of his energy to reinforcing the pair bond, to avoid being cuckolded by another male.

The breeding season is a tough time for birds: males often become exhausted by their tasks of defending a territory, winning and keeping a mate, and then raising a family. Yet the drive to breed overcomes all this.

Right: *Once the young have hatched, the parent Wrens are kept very busy, finding caterpillars and other titbits to feed their hungry chicks. These young birds are almost ready to fledge and leave the safety of their nest.*

Nest-building

Once the pair bond has been formed, the next stage in the breeding process is to build a nest. This isn't as easy as it sounds: male Wrens often build a number of nests and show the choosy female around each one before she finally decides where to lay her eggs. Other birds will begin to build a nest, then give up, possibly because the immediate area is subject to disturbance. The choice of nest site is a crucial one and not to be undertaken lightly.

In early spring (from about February onwards), watch out for birds carrying material

Above: In early spring, look out for birds such as this Starling collecting and carrying material with which they will build their nests.

Below: House Martins fill their beaks with tiny globules of mud, which they take back to their nest-site in order to build their cup-shaped nests under the eaves of a house.

such as straw or dried grass in their bills. They may head for a particular bush, or part of a hedge, deposit the material then head off for some more, a sure sign that they are nest-building. If you can, resist the chance to peek, as this is the time when they are most likely to give up and go somewhere else.

The same applies to hole-nesting birds such as tits, which may be prospecting a natural hole in a tree or looking inside one of your nestboxes.

Egg-laying and incubation

Once the nest has been built, it's time for the female to lay her eggs. The size of the clutch may vary from just one or two, in the case of pigeons or doves, to as many as ten or even a dozen (several species of tit). Eggs are usually laid on a daily basis, and incubation does not begin until the clutch is complete, so that the eggs all hatch at roughly the same time.

The time spent incubating also varies from species to species and family to family. Pied Wagtail's eggs may hatch after just 11 days, while the eggs of most songbirds take from two to three weeks to hatch. This is the time when you may not see the adult birds very much, as the female is usually sitting tight, while the male visits infrequently so as not to reveal the whereabouts of the nest to predators. Some species share the duties of incubation, while in the case of others these are confined to the long-suffering female.

Chick development

When the eggs finally hatch, things really start to hot up. The parents must now spend every waking moment finding food to bring back to feed their hungry young. This may not be easy, especially at times when bad weather restricts the hours available for feeding; so, by putting out food at this time of year, you are providing a valuable lifeline to help the birds.

The young of most songbirds hatch blind and virtually naked apart from a sparse covering of down, so are

Above: *Starlings lay between four and seven pale blue, glossy eggs in a cup-shaped nest made from straw and grass, lined with feathers.*

Below: *Once the eggs have hatched, parent birds, such as this Song Thrush, spend every waking hour between dawn and dusk collecting food to bring back to their hungry brood.*

entirely dependent on their parents at this stage in their lives. As well as being fed, they must also be kept warm, usually by being brooded by whichever parent is not finding food. As they begin to grow bigger, and more capable of looking after themselves in the nest, both parents will leave to seek food.

Rapidly – usually within a week or two – the baby birds will grow more and more like their parents, shedding their down and producing 'proper' feathers. After sometime between eight days (some warblers) and five weeks (larger species such as pigeons) they will 'fledge': having gained their full feathers they will leave the nest and begin to learn to fend for themselves.

Multiple broods

For the parents, the busy time may have just begun. As well as looking after their newly fledged brood of chicks,

Above: *After leaving the nest Long-tailed Tits stay together in family parties for some weeks or even months, searching for food and roosting for the night together.*

some species will raise one, two, three or even four further broods of chicks.

Not all garden birds are multiple brooded. Most kinds of tit, for instance, raise only a single brood, devoting their time and energy to making sure that they raise the maximum number of chicks from that one, and often helping the young to find food long after they have left the nest.

Neither of these strategies is necessarily better than the other: birds do what has suited them over generations of evolution, though if conditions should change (e.g. with global warming allowing a longer breeding season) some species may switch from being single to multiple brooded over time.

WHAT TO DO IF YOU FIND A BABY BIRD

Every June, July and August the RSPB headquarters at Sandy in Bedfordshire receives hundreds – sometimes thousands – of telephone calls and letters asking one simple question: 'I've found a baby bird that has fallen out of its nest. What should I do with it?'

The answer is, quite simply, nothing. The worst thing that you can do is to pick up the bird and bring it into the house: you will almost certainly be causing its death. That's because it probably hasn't fallen out of its nest, but instead has just fledged and left the nest of its own accord (or been pushed by its parents). The adult birds are usually quite close, and it is the presence of a human being that is stopping them from getting on with the task of feeding the baby bird.

The only exception to this is if you find an unfeathered nestling that is clearly still naked, blind and helpless, directly beneath a nest. In this case, it *has* fallen out; and if it is still alive you should put it back into the nest as quickly as possible and hope for the best. If not, its fate is sealed, as it will not be able to survive exposure to the elements. In such cases, the only humane alternative is to kill the nestling as quickly as possible.

If you find a baby bird and are still really unsure what to do, then contact the RSPB Enquiry Unit on 01767 680551. But be patient – you may have to wait for an answer if the phones are very busy. Another possibility is to call your local Wildlife Trust, who will be able to offer you advice.

Below: *Young Robins are fed by their parents for some time after leaving the nest, and moult from their drab juvenile plumage into their bright adult garb only after several months. If you find a young bird on your lawn, stay away and watch – its parent will probably soon return to feed it.*

Moulting

For many birds, the breeding season is more or less over by July or August. At this point, the adults are worn and tatty, having spent so much time feeding their hungry young that they have neglected to maintain their plumage in good condition. Most songbirds take advantage of the abundance of natural food resources and go into moult, replacing their old, worn feathers with spanking new ones. This may take several weeks, during which time they hide away so as to avoid the danger from predators. Summer is also a good time because there is plenty of foliage in which to conceal themselves and there is no danger of succumbing to cold during the period when new feathers are being grown.

Moult is essential for both resident birds and migrants. Residents must have their plumage in tip-top condition in order to resist the hardships of the coming winter; while migrants require their feathers to work perfectly as they prepare to fly perhaps many thousands of miles on their arduous journey to their winter quarters.

Juvenile birds (i.e. those hatched this year) also moult in late summer or early autumn, usually acquiring the same plumage as their parents.

Above: *Juvenile Starlings moult gradually into full adult plumage, acquiring spots on the flanks and belly first. At this time they may be hard to identify.*

Below: *This juvenile Green Woodpecker has begun the process of moulting into full adult plumage, gradually acquiring its bright green plumage and red head.*

Flocking

By late summer or early autumn, many species of bird are beginning to form flocks. They do so for a number of reasons: primarily because, for each individual bird, being in a flock offers a greater chance of finding food than foraging by themselves; but also because being part of a larger congregation of birds gives them a much better chance of avoiding being caught and killed by a predator. Additionally, on a cold winter's night, being in a flock gives each bird a better chance of surviving, as they are able to huddle together and gain warmth from their neighbours.

Some species, such as Starlings, form vast flocks, which can be seen wheeling around against the evening sky at specific sites. Others, such as Pied Wagtails, gather in flocks of 50 or 100 birds, often choosing a favourite tree or bush in which to spend the night.

Tit flocks are one of the most obvious manifestations of flocking behaviour. From autumn onwards, you will hear the high-pitched calls that draw attention to the presence of a small party of tits. Often these are mixed up of several species, including the common Blue, Great, Coal and Long-tailed Tits, but also with the occasional scarcer species such as Marsh or Willow Tits, or even a Treecreeper or Lesser Spotted Woodpecker tagging along behind. Tit flocks work their way around a circuit of several gardens, spending some time on feeders, and the rest of their energy searching amongst twigs and branches for tiny morsels of food to keep their energy levels up.

Above: *Magpies are sociable birds, and their habit of forming flocks has often been celebrated in rhyme and folklore. In this case the line is 'four for a boy'!*

Left: *In winter, small birds such as tits and Goldcrests join together in order to seek out scarce food resources.*

Flight-lines

During the autumn and winter, larger birds also form loose flocks, especially in the evening and early morning when going to and from their roosting places. If you live on a flight-path or flight-line you can watch the spectacle of hundreds, sometimes even thousands, of birds as they pass overhead. Gulls are the commonest species in many areas, especially if you live near a reservoir or flooded gravel-pit where they go to roost for the night. They may also be joined by crows, Rooks and Jackdaws, whose presence is given away by their distinctive calls. Other birds that regularly fly over gardens in flocks include thrushes, especially Fieldfare and Redwing (and, where I live in West London, parakeets).

If you are planning to watch a flight-line, wrap up warmly and find a prominent place in your garden from which you can get a good view of the skies around you. If you are so inclined, you may want to count the birds as they pass: but be prepared to do some 'guesstimating' when larger flocks come over. And don't give up at dusk: birds will stay on to feed as long as they can, especially in cold weather, so the largest flocks may pass over when it is almost dark.

Above: *At dawn and dusk, on autumn and winter days look out for flocks of gulls travelling from their roosts to their daytime feeding grounds.*

Below: *Jackdaws are another species that regularly travels to and from its roost in large flocks, often calling as they go.*

RECORDING GARDEN BIRDS

Keeping a record of the birds you see in, around and over your garden is not merely for your own benefit: it may also be useful for their conservation. Projects like the BTO Garden BirdWatch (see below) use the data collected by ordinary people up and down the country to find out more about changes in our common bird populations and thereby help to conserve them.

I keep a small A5 notebook handy to note down sightings of birds in the garden: different species, times and numbers of birds; unusual behaviour; and counts of flocks. After just four months in a new home, it makes fascinating reading, and spurs me to watch more often than I might otherwise.

You can decide how detailed you want your notes to be, but I would suggest keeping a record of at least the following points:

- The various different species (you can count those that fly overhead if you can identify them with certainty).
- Dates, times, and the number of individual bird seen.
- Specific behaviour (especially unusual events).
- What the birds are feeding on (this will help you adjust your feeding programme to suit the birds).

If you plan to keep regular records of your garden birds, you should also join the BTO's Garden BirdWatch Survey. You will be sent a recording form on which you note down a weekly record of the species and numbers of birds visiting your garden. The BTO then processes the data and sends you a regular newsletter giving details of changes in trends, unusual sightings, and so on.

To take part, contact the BTO on 01842 750050 and ask for Garden BirdWatch. There is a registration fee to cover costs.

Above: *Finding a garden rarity, such as this once-common Tree Sparrow, is definitely something worth recording. Note when and where you saw it and what it was doing.*

Below: *Keeping field notes allows you to identify unfamiliar birds such as this Brambling. The details here enable anyone to tell it apart from the more common Chaffinch.*

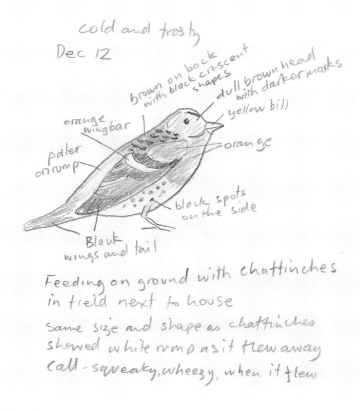

Climate Change and Garden Birds

No-one could fail to be aware that we are currently undergoing a major change in climate, which could have a significant effect on the behaviour of our garden birds. Indeed, it already has. A few years ago, BTO researchers, using records collected by amateur birdwatchers, discovered an astonishing fact. They found that many common British breeding birds were now beginning to build nests and lay eggs up to two weeks earlier, on average, than 30 years ago. This change in behaviour was undoubtedly the result of the effects of global warming, which has brought the start date of spring earlier by two or even three weeks in some parts of the United Kingdom.

Left: *Climate change may bring warmer summers, allowing continental European birds such as the exotic Bee-eater to breed in southern Britain.*

Below: *On the other hand, it may also bring milder winters, encouraging winter visitors from the north and east such as this male Brambling to stay closer to their breeding grounds for the winter.*

In the short term, this appears to be good news for our garden birds, as it gives them a greater chance of raising larger broods and more young. But, in the longer term, it could prove disastrous. Breeding birds rely on being in close synchronisation with their prey species, so when baby Blue Tits hatch there is normally a large number of caterpillars available for them to be fed on. If global warming continues to move the goalposts, however, different organisms will respond in different ways, so that the breeding cycle of a bird could very soon become out of synchrony with its main food supply.

Moreover, most migrants begin their journeys to and from their winter quarters in response to changes in day-length rather than temperature. If they continue to return at the same time as they always have, they may also find that the food supply that they rely on is no longer available. They will also be competing with resident species that have had the advantage of starting the breeding season earlier than before.

Migrants suffer from global warming in other ways, too. More severe droughts in Africa could affect their wintering grounds and stopover places; while increased storminess, especially at the spring and autumn equinoxes, may also reduce their chances of making a successful journey.

Winter visitors, such as Redwings, Fieldfares and Bramblings, may become increasingly scarce in Britain, if mild weather on the Continent means they can stay put rather than migrate.

In the longer term, global warming is bound to have an effect on the distribution of some of our common species. Birds such as Marsh Tit, currently confined as a British breeder to England and Wales, may spread north to colonize parts of Scotland. Small birds, such as the Wren, should see population booms, thanks to a reduced death

Above: *Recent warming has allowed several continental European species such as the Golden Oriole to breed in Britain. On the continent this is a regular garden bird.*

rate because of fewer harsh winters. And feral species such as Rose-ringed Parakeet (and other escaped cagebirds) could enjoy a bonanza thanks to milder winters and the greater availability of food. Finally, we could even see new arrivals such as the Hoopoe, Black Kite and Bee-eater, all of which are potential colonists to our shores.

The Garden Bird Year

The aim of this chapter is to show the various changes that occur in the average garden during the 12 months of the year. These include the cycle of the seasons, the effects of the changing weather, major changes such as migration and breeding, and smaller but just as interesting shifts in the pattern of visits from different bird species.

Depending upon where you live, these changes may happen earlier or later than outlined here, but this calendar should give you an idea of what to look out for and to expect. Always bear in mind that the bird's seasons are very different from our own, and that what may appear to be unusual behaviour for a particular time of year (e.g. birdsong in February) may, for some species, be perfectly normal.

Every keen gardener knows that one of the most interesting aspects to their hobby is the way that different seasons bring new things to see. The bird gardener is no exception: indeed, one of the most fascinating aspects of gardening for birds is that every month is different, bringing new arrivals, seeing other birds depart, and watching the different kinds of bird behaviour.

This chapter is designed to enable you to know what to look out for from month to month. Do remember, however, that the seasons may vary from year to year, or depending whether you live in the north or south of the country. Nevertheless, this should serve as a general guide to what to expect during the twelve months of the garden bird year.

Left: *Spring is a wonderful time in the garden, as birds like this Blue Tit pose on a blossom covered tree.*

Above: *Winter is a tough time for garden birds. This Chaffinch is searching for food amongst the snow.*

Right: *In summer, newly fledged Wrens often stick together in family groups for some time after leaving the nest.*

Above: *January is a good month to look out for flocks of Waxwings, which often gorge themselves on berry bushes before moving on.*

January

New Year is upon us again and it is time to make all those resolutions. As well as thinking of yourself, why not include the birds too? If you don't do so already, you could start by keeping a diary of all the birds that you see in your garden, including numbers and details of interesting or unusual behaviour. This is for your entertainment and interest, so what you include is up to you.

Another important resolution can be summed up in the famous *Mastermind* catchphrase, 'I've started, so I'll finish...' If you have made up your mind to feed the birds in your garden this year, you can't be half-hearted about it. Once they have discovered a food source, birds soon come to rely upon it, regularly visiting your garden feeders on their daily circuit. If you fail to put out food, they will waste valuable time without reward. At this time of year, when natural food resources are scarce and daylight hours are limited, providing a regular, reliable supply of food is especially important.

Pecking order

The phrase 'pecking order' originally referred to the complex feeding behaviour of domestic chickens, where the dominant hen will feed before her less-pushy subordinates. But the phrase can also be applied to the birds that visit your garden to feed. By and large, the bigger the bird the higher it comes in the pecking order, but there are exceptions to this rule.

Starlings are particularly aggressive and dominant, especially on birdtables and feeders, often ejecting all-comers, whether or not they are bigger or smaller. Amongst the tit family, Great Tits are, as you would expect, the dominant ones, with Blue and then Coal Tits nipping in to grab a seed or piece of peanut as and when they can. House Sparrows tend to kick off Robins, while Dunnocks

THINGS TO DO

- Start off the New Year by reviewing your garden and planning what to do in the year to come.
- Finish off any pruning or tidying up from the previous autumn. Don't leave this until later in the year – the birds will be nesting.
- Check every morning to make sure your birdbath is ice-free. If not, de-ice it with a pan of hot water (see page 27).

opt out altogether by creeping around beneath the feeders or bird-table, picking up the crumbs.

If you are really lucky, you may get regular visits from Great Spotted Woodpeckers, which are big and powerful enough to ignore any other birds on the feeder.

Flight-lines

January is a good month to watch flocks of birds going to roost, generally in the hour or so around dusk. If you are lucky enough to live on a flight-line, you may see quite large numbers of gulls, pigeons and crows, as they pass overhead on their way to roost for the night. This is a good opportunity to improve your identification skills, both of birds in flight (and often in silhouette) and of their calls. Many birds, such as the different kinds of gull, can be told apart by their distinctive flight shape and action; while Jackdaws and Rooks are best identified by a combination of appearance and their distinctive calls. Other birds which regular fly to roost in flocks include Lapwings, thrushes (including Fieldfare and Redwing) and, in parts of suburban London, exotic Rose-ringed Parakeets, which give away their presence by a high-pitched, screeching call.

If you wish, you can keep regular records of numbers of birds passing overhead. The best way to do this is to watch from a particular place in your home or garden, for a defined length of time (say the half-hour before dusk). You will be amazed at the sheer numbers of birds that can pass overhead, especially if you live near a reservoir, flooded gravel-pit, wood or other regular roosting site. If you do keep records, make sure that you send them in to your county bird recorder or local bird club.

Above: *January sees large flocks of winter thrushes such as Fieldfares in Britain – if the weather is harsh then they will often visit gardens in search of food.*

Right: *The Robin is the classic winter bird in gardens, often becoming very tame, especially if you dig up the soil in order to allow it to feed on worms and beetles.*

Above: *February sees the highest mortality in small songbirds such as this Greenfinch, which rely on food put out by garden owners in order to survive.*

Below: *Coal Tits are regular garden visitors for some; for others the best bet is when harsh winter weather means that food supplies in the wider countryside are scarce, so they need to visit gardens.*

February

Although January is statistically the coldest month of the year, February is often the time when the cumulative effects of freezing weather lead to severe food shortages for small birds. Even a day or two without enough food can lead to rapid starvation, as their metabolism is so high that they need constantly to renew their energy.

So, more than ever, now is the time to put out regular and sufficient quantities of food, especially energy-rich items such as sunflower seeds and peanuts. You may need to refill your feeders daily, and make sure that you also save any kitchen scraps such as stale bread and fruit to put on your birdtable.

February is an excellent month to spend time really watching your garden birds: observing minute details of their behaviour and looking out for surprises.

Unusual visitors

Cold weather may drive some unusual visitors out of the surrounding woods, fields and parks and into the sanctuary of your garden. Great and Blue Tits are regular visitors to virtually every garden in the country and are often joined by their less colourful cousin, the Coal Tit. A spell of snow and ice may also bring Marsh Tit, or, if you are really lucky, Willow Tit, to your feeders, though both these similar, black-capped species have declined in recent years, and Willow Tit in particular is now quite a rare and localized breeding bird. Neither of these species is found very far north in Britain. Scottish garden owners may, however, be lucky enough to enjoy a visit from the rarest British tit of all, the Crested Tit. These delightful birds are confined to a few well-wooded areas of the Scottish highlands, with their stronghold in the Spey Valley. Like other members of their family, they have adapted to visiting tit-feeders, and may be seen jostling for position with their cousins.

Other unusual winter visitors may include the two winter thrushes (Redwing and Fieldfare), Nuthatch or Treecreeper; or perhaps a woodpecker or two; all attracted by the prospect of easy pickings from your garden.

Spring is on its way

February is not all doom and gloom. Harsh though the winter weather may be, there is often a change in the wind, bringing milder air from the southwest, or in recent years even a touch of early spring weather from the near-Continent. During such conditions, temperatures may reach the high teens Celsius, more typical of April or May than midwinter.

Warmer temperatures, together with the rapidly increasing hours of daylight and consequent lighter evenings, bring another spring-like phenomenon: the start of birdsong. Of course, some birds (notably the Robin) sing throughout the winter, but, for others, spring must be in the air before they begin. Amongst the first to start singing in earnest are two members of the thrush family: Song Thrush and Blackbird. Both are early breeders, often building their nests and laying eggs as early as March, so time is of the essence if they are to establish a territory and win a mate.

So, as you walk home from work or finish off some tasks in the garden on a mild February afternoon, listen out for the unmistakable sound of a Song Thrush pouring out its wonderful song, full of repeated phrases as if it wanted to emphasize its message. Blackbirds, too, have a very distinctive song: less repetitive and more fluty than that of the Song Thrush. If you have mature trees in your garden, or live near a park, you may also hear the song of the largest member of the family, the Mistle Thrush. In some ways, this sounds like a cross between the song of its cousins: deep and fluty like that of the Blackbird and with regular repeated phrases like that of the Song Thrush.

Above right: *The Crested Tit is Britain's rarest tit species, found only in a small part of the Scottish pine forests. However, in this area it is quite tame and often visits garden birdfeeders, especially in winter.*

Right: *Britain's largest species of thrush, the Mistle Thrush is also one of our earliest breeding birds, sometimes starting to sing its loud, powerful song in late February.*

THINGS TO DO

- Listen out for the first singing bird of each species, and note down the date in your records.
- Top up your nut and seed feeders as often as possible, especially during hard weather.
- Put out some old fruit, such as apples or pears, on your lawn or birdtable for winter thrushes.

March

March is the month when the resident breeding birds really get going. By now, all will be in song and on fine early mornings your garden will echo to the chorus of an undisciplined orchestra, as each bird attempts to outdo not only its fellow vocalists, but any background noise from cars, trains or aeroplanes. It is well worth rising early one morning to hear the dawn chorus at its best.

The loudest song comes from the smallest bird: the Wren, whose accelerated crescendo followed by a scolding trill is one of the most distinctive sounds of any garden. Wrens have enjoyed a population boom in recent years, thanks to the run of mild winters caused by global warming. So, if there has been another snow-free season, your garden may play host to more than one male singing for all he is worth.

A quieter, but just as persistent, songster is easier to see at this time of year than at any other. Dunnocks are normally skulking creatures, creeping and shuffling about on the ground beneath the shrubbery in search of tiny morsels of food. In early spring, however, they are transformed into proud solo singers, often perching on top of a bush or tree to deliver their song. Unfortunately, this is almost as dull as their brown and grey plumage: a reticent jumble of seemingly unconnected notes with little or no structure, which just seems to begin and end at random moments.

Above: *Britain's commonest breeding bird, with more than seven million pairs, the Wren is unobtrusive for much of the year. However, in March it often sings its loud, penetrating song from prominent perches.*

Left: *Blackbirds are another early breeder, often starting to sing early in the New Year. In March, most males have begun to defend a territory against all-comers, often singing at dawn and again at dusk.*

The March Nightingale

If anyone tells you that they have a Nightingale singing in their garden, the chances are that it is a Robin or perhaps a Blackbird. But in March, there's a chance that it may be a Blackcap, a robust member of the warbler family that arrives back to our shores earlier than most of its relatives. The poet John Clare called this bird the March Nightingale, because it sounds similar to the better-known songster (which does not arrive back from its African winter-quarters until late April or early May).

The other warbler that often arrives back in March is the Chiffchaff: a tiny, leaf-like bird with the unmistakable song that gives the species its name. Listen out for the song of the Chiffchaff anytime from the beginning of the month.

Some lucky people have Blackcaps in their garden throughout the winter. These, however, are not our British breeding birds that have decided to spend the winter season with us, but are immigrants from Central Europe. Blackcaps from Germany and Austria have changed their migratory habits in recent years, choosing to spend the winter in the relatively mild climate of our suburban gardens, rather than heading off on a longer journey to Spain or North Africa. Superficially, they may be confused with another black-capped species, the Marsh Tit; but on closer inspection the larger size, grey plumage and long, fine bill of the Blackcap make identification relatively easy.

THINGS TO DO

- Listen for any new singers in your garden: especially early migrants.
- Watch out for birds beginning to collect nesting material such as twigs, feathers, moss, bark, even bits of paper.
- Discreetly keep an eye on your nestboxes for any nesting activity.

GREENFINCHES AND GREEN FINCHES

Not every green finch that you see in your garden is actually a Greenfinch. Another member of the finch family that has become a regular garden visitor in recent years is the Siskin. Smaller than its commoner relative, with substantial black streaking and a deeply forked tail, Siskins began coming to peanut feeders on a regular basis two or three decades ago. The trend caught on, and most rural or large suburban gardens now enjoy visits from this delightful little finch.

March is one of the peak times for Siskin visits, as food in surrounding woodlands is now scarce, and they need to build up fuel reserves as many will soon migrate northwards to breed in Scotland or Scandinavia. Try putting out red feeders, as this seems to be the birds' preferred colour, probably because it reminds them of their natural food of alder cones.

Right: *Siskins can be easily told apart from their close relative the Greenfinch by their smaller size, and black on head, wings and tail.*

April

April is one of the most exciting months in the garden, with resident species reaching the peak of their breeding season. At the same time, new arrivals get ready to make the most of their short window of opportunity provided by the long daylight hours of the northern summer. Many summer visitors are familiar garden birds, with House Martins virtually dependent on human dwellings on which to construct their nests. Others, such as Willow Warbler and Whitethroat, are not really garden birds at all, but may breed in larger, more rural gardens.

For breeding birds, April's weather can be critical. A sudden cold snap with ice and snow, or prolonged rain, can spell disaster for newly laid clutches of eggs or just-hatched chicks. Cold and wet weather may chill eggs beyond recovery, so that they will never hatch, and chicks suffer both from the direct effects of poor weather and its indirect ones such as lack of food.

So, more than ever, make sure that you do not allow the food that you supply for the birds to tail off at this important time of year. Water, too, is vital, as feeding

Above: *The Whitethroat arrives in mid- to late April, and often sings by launching itself into the air and uttering a series of fast, scratchy notes.*

young chicks can be thirsty work. If you keep a regular log of visitors to your garden, April is likely to be the month when you add the most new species: not just visitors to the garden itself, but also those flying overhead on their way to breed elsewhere.

New arrivals

Some species, such as House Martin and Swallow, are obviously new arrivals in the area at this time of year, as their wintering grounds are thousands of miles to the south, in sub-Saharan Africa. But other spring visitors may also have travelled, albeit not quite so far. Birds such as Goldfinches undertake movements in autumn and winter to avoid the harsh effects of the weather; and the majority of the British breeding population actually spends the winter in Belgium, France or even Spain. They return in April and May, often visiting gardens in order to replenish their reserves of energy before settling down to breed.

THINGS TO DO

- Consider changing to 'summer foods' recommended by some bird-food dealers, or change to sunflower seeds.
- Watch out for returning summer migrants such as the first swallows, martins and swifts.
- Give House Martins a helping hand by putting up artificial nextboxes under your eaves.
- Keep your birdbath and birdtable clean, to maintain good hygiene.

Other short-distance migrants include the Song Thrush, many of which also spend the winter on the Continent; while its close relative the Redwing will now be heading away from Britain to its breeding grounds in Scandinavia and northern Europe.

Nestboxes and natural holes

At this time of year, with the breeding season well under way, nest sites may be at a premium. With luck, this means that the nestbox that you put up last autumn will now be occupied, probably by a pair of Blue or Great Tits, or possibly by a family of House Sparrows. As you watch the birds come and go, it can be tempting to make regular checks inside the box to monitor progress. Be warned, however, that your actions may cause the birds to desert and abandon their breeding attempt, especially early on in the process. Far better to be patient and wait a week or so until the pair has really settled in before checking; and even then, do so only occasionally and as quickly and carefully as you can manage.

Other birds, including all three species of woodpecker, Stock Doves, Starlings, Jackdaws and the newly established Rose-ringed Parakeet, prefer to nest in natural holes. If you have large, mature trees in your garden, keep a close eye out for prospecting birds. Some, such as the parakeets, are noisy and obvious, whilst others, including the rare Lesser Spotted Woodpecker, are so unobtrusive that it is easy to miss them. If you have a telescope, it may be worth setting it up so that you can watch the entrance hole to a nest to get fabulous close-up views of the adults' comings and goings.

Above: *Goldfinches are a regular garden visitor in the month of April, before they join up in pairs and settle down to breed.*

Right: *Spring is a good time to search for the elusive Lesser Spotted Woodpecker, our smallest woodpecker species, as it may be more active during courtship and breeding.*

May

May is a wonderful month in which to enjoy the birds in your garden, with the maximum diversity of species now that all the summer visitors have arrived. Activity is non-stop, as parent birds search frantically for items of food to satisfy the constant demands of their hungry chicks. In between, the males still somehow find time to sing in defence of their territory, especially at dawn and dusk, when the chorus can seem overwhelming.

The first baby birds now appear, perhaps perched on your garden fence or sitting in the middle of the lawn. They may appear helpless, but by and large their parents know where they are and are able to look after them and feed them in the few days before they grow large enough to fend for themselves.

Fine evenings see the first gatherings of Swallows, martins and Swifts, hawking for insects high in the sky; a sure sign that summer is just around the corner.

Late arrivals

Some summer visitors, such as the Blackcap and the Chiffchaff, arrive back to our shores as early as March in

THINGS TO DO

- Get up early one morning and enjoy the dawn chorus.
- Put out live food such as mealworms to help supplement breeding birds' diets. Adult birds will be so busy providing food for their young, that they themselves could be undernourished.
- Fill in a nest record card for every bird nesting in your garden (contact BTO for details).

order to get going on their breeding programme. But others wait until the middle or even the end of May before returning. These include three species that, if you are very lucky, may be regular or occasional visitors to your garden.

The first is the Cuckoo, a bird which everyone knows about and which most people have heard, but which very few of us actually get to see. Because of their habit of laying their eggs in other birds' nests, Cuckoos are furtive in their behaviour. Males may sing from a perch, but more often than not are hidden away in the foliage, with only

Left: *House Martins start to arrive in April, but the bulk of the birds return from their African winter quarters in early May, bringing a touch of summer to our towns and suburbs.*

the unmistakable sound giving away their presence. The female's song is much less well known: a bubbling call, quite unlike her mate's 'Cuck-oo'.

Turtle Doves also have a distinctive call, which, like that of the male Cuckoo, gives the bird its unusual name: 'turtle' is a corruption of the 'tur-tur' sound made by this delightful little dove. In recent years, it has become increasingly rare, due to a combination of shooting abroad and poor breeding seasons at home; indeed you are much more likely to hear and see their upstart relative, the Collared Dove, nowadays.

Finally, a much more typical garden bird, especially if you have a large, rural garden with stone or brick walls: the Spotted Flycatcher. This bird lives up to its name in two senses: it has a finely spotted plumage and it catches flies with great skill, launching itself off a perch with a flurry of wings to seize its prey. It is a regular garden breeder throughout Britain, though, like the Turtle Dove, it has suffered a recent population decline. They will nest in nestboxes, and in climbing plants.

Above: *The Spotted Flycatcher is one of our latest summer migrants, usually returning in mid-May, and sallying forth from a high perch to catch insects in its bill.*

THE DEVIL BIRDS

On a fine evening in May, if you live in a town or city, you will hear the sound that more than any other typifies the urban summer. A thin, piercing, high-pitched scream, which signals that the Swifts have arrived back from their winter-quarters in Africa to reclaim their place in the skies above our homes.

Swifts generally arrive back in late April or early May and seem to appear in huge numbers as if from nowhere: one day they are nowhere to be seen, then the next day there are dozens of them above every city, town and village. Farther north, they may not arrive until mid- or even late May; but once here they provide a constant soundtrack for the summer season.

Swifts have a special place in country folklore, with their screams said to be those of dead souls in torment, earning them the nickname of 'devil bird'. They have some pretty bizarre habits, too: feeding and even sleeping on the wing and never landing on the ground: the ultimate flying machine.

Above: *Swifts are the true sound of summer in many urban parts of Britain: in city centres they may be one of the few breeding species.*

June

Flaming June sees the longest day of the year, which in northern Britain means that it hardly gets dark at all, and even in southern parts of the country the birds have at least 16 hours a day to forage for food for their growing young. Yet, as the month progresses, things can begin to turn rather quiet. Partly this is an illusion, caused by the growth of foliage, so that you may not always be able to see everything that is going on, but partly it is real. For many resident species, the bulk of the breeding season is over and males no longer feel the need to sing to defend their hard-won territories. Keep a close eye on your birdbath or pond – there is a fair amount of bird activity around water, since the warmer weather will mean that the birds need to drink and bathe more.

Right: *June is a month full of activity: this Great Tit is feeding a small caterpillar to its newly-fledged young. Later they will learn to fend for themselves.*

Below: *The young Blackbird (left) is still dependent on its parent (male, right), despite being almost as big!*

Not all birds are putting their feet up, however. Some species, including Song Thrush and Blackbird, continue raising new broods of youngsters so long as food is available for them to do so. For both species, up to four or even five broods in a single season have been recorded.

You should notice far more young birds at this time of year. They are usually easily told apart from their parents by their fresher plumage (often more closely resembling that of the dowdy female than the showy male), and often the tell-tale remains of the yellow mark at the sides of their beak, which stimulates the parent to go on providing food by drawing attention to the gape.

Baby birds

For a few weeks at this time of year, The Wildlife Trusts receive hundreds of enquiries asking the same question: 'I've found a baby bird that has been abandoned by its parents. What should I do?' (see page 61).

This is the time of year when young birds are leaving the nest. Most baby songbirds leave the nest at the point of fledging, when they are only just able to fly and fend for themselves. As a result, the parents (or sometimes older siblings from previous broods) will look after the youngster. This may not, however, always be obvious to the casual onlooker, and the baby bird may appear to have been callously abandoned. The best thing to do if you find a bird like this is to retreat to a safe distance and watch. Once the coast is clear, the parents will almost certainly resume feeding the chick.

Cats

June is, not surprisingly, a bumper month for the neighbourhood cats, which find the surplus of baby birds easy pickings. In some ways this is not as bad as it looks, since the vast majority of young birds will die during their first year of life anyway, so the species' population is unlikely to be greatly affected. Nevertheless, it is unpleasant and upsetting to find tiny corpses of birds all over your garden; and it has the knock-on effect of deterring birds from breeding there. So during June be extra vigilant, and if you are a cat-owner yourself, please ensure that your cat has a bell on its collar to warn the birds and give them a sporting chance of escape.

THINGS TO DO

- On fine evenings sit out in the garden and watch Swifts, House Martins and perhaps Sand Martins hunting overhead.
- As the weather gets warmer, put out more water in your birdbath so that it doesn't run out, or become stagnant. Rainwater is best.
- If you find a baby bird, don't do anything until you've checked with the RSPB Enquiry Unit (see page 61 and Useful Addresses).
- Supply food as you have been doing, but you can reduce the quantities somewhat as natural food is more readily available in your garden.
- If you are a cat owner, or your neighbours are, fit the cat with a bell on its collar to warn the birds of their approach.

Below: *Bullfinches are a rare garden visitor, as they are generally very shy birds. However, in hot summer weather they may take advantage of a supply of water, such as your pond, in a rural garden. Keep your pond topped up with water almost daily, so that it does not become stagnant.*

July

July is a funny month. It can be one of the quietest times in the garden, as many birds have finished breeding and the adults have begun the process of moult, so they hide away from predators. On the other hand, some species are quite visible, as they rove around in family parties searching for food. Birdsong has more or less finished, but some species will continue singing from time to time, in a desultory defence of their territory.

A puzzling feature of July can be the appearance of birds with unusual plumages in the garden. Young Blue and Great Tits are easy to identify, as apart from yellow cheeks they are more or less the same as their parents; but you may come across a bird that, although shaped like a Robin, has a drab, spotty plumage with no hint of a red breast. It is, of course, simply a juvenile Robin: a bird hatched a few weeks earlier, which has yet to acquire the smart plumage of its parents through the process of moult, which will take place later in the autumn.

Another nice feature of July is the appearance of other wildlife in the garden. If you have planted plenty of nectar-bearing plants you should be rewarded with plenty of butterflies, especially on warm, sunny days. Mammals such as Hedgehogs and Red Foxes (and, if you are really lucky, Badgers) are also very active on warm summer evenings. Your garden may also be home to many small mammals such as voles and shrews, but these are rarely seen.

Summer droughts

The British summer weather is notoriously fickle and spells of prolonged rain and wind can spell disaster for breeding birds, as young fail to get enough food to maintain crucial energy levels. Fine weather can, however, also bring problems, in the shape of prolonged drought. Long spells with little or no rain mean that some insects, such as caterpillars, may become very scarce, leading to food shortages for birds that depend on them to feed their young.

Birds such as the Song Thrush and the Blackbird, which regularly feed on open lawns, can also face problems. Dry conditions make the ground hard and force earthworms and other invertebrates to burrow deep under ground, far out of reach of these birds' beaks. So, make sure that you provide a top-up food resource, perhaps in the form of mealworms.

Water is also crucial, especially on hot, sunny days, when birds can dehydrate rapidly. Insect eaters get much of their moisture from their food, but seedeaters, such as sparrows and finches, need regular drinks in order to digest their food. Bathing is also important, as hot weather can increase the spread of feather parasites, such as lice; so make sure that you keep your birdbath regularly topped up with fresh, clean water.

Left: *A newly fledged juvenile Robin is an odd-looking bird: only its size and shape enable you to tell that it is related to its brightly-coloured parents.*

THINGS TO DO

- Check your pond for algal blooms, which may cause stagnation. Clean them out with a sieve and return any creatures you pick up to the pond.
- Reduce your food supplies and clean up waste food every day or two.
- Clean your birdbath regularly to reduce risk of disease.

Above: *On a hot, sunny summer's afternoon look out for birds such as this Song Thrush sunbathing. Watch how it spreads out its feathers to catch the full warmth of the sun.*

Below: *In very hot summer weather make sure that your garden pond doesn't become stagnant by clearing algae off the surface using a sieve or saucepan.*

Garden ponds

You also need to keep a close eye on your garden pond, if you have one. Ponds can rapidly become clogged with algae, especially during hot weather, when it spreads across the surface very rapidly. Make sure that you regularly clear the surface using a small net; and to fight the effects of algae it is important to have a good supply of submerged and floating plants, especially those that provide supplies of oxygen into the water. Without these, your pond runs the risk of becoming not only stagnant and smelly, but also no good at all for your garden birds.

Also, if the level of water in your pond is dropping, make sure you keep it topped up, preferably with rain-water or water from a larger pond owned by a neighbour.

August

It may not feel like autumn yet, but for many birds the summer (and breeding season) is now well over and they are beginning to change their lifestyles in preparation for the autumn and winter to come. August is a quiet month in the garden: food is abundant and many birds leave to explore the surrounding habitats.

Birds may be in family parties at this time of year: the adults still looking very tatty until their moult period is over and they reappear in their splendid new finery. A few species will still be hard at work raising new broods, but, by and large, the nesting season is over again for another year.

August is a good time for unusual visitors to the garden: perhaps a Sparrowhawk, Little Owl or Tawny Owl, which have now finished breeding and may roam around the area. Even if these less-common visitors fail to put in an appearance, there is always something to see: either the antics of a family party of Greenfinches on your feeders, or the elegant behaviour of Collared Doves as they warily search for food.

Above: *Late summer is a good time to look out for unusual garden visitors such as this Little Owl, which may wander after finishing breeding.*

Disease and hygiene

Heat breeds disease, so, during long periods of fine, hot weather, make sure that you keep your birdtable and feeders as clean as possible; removing uneaten food every few days

LOOK UP!

If you live in the south of England, it's worth looking up at this time of year, especially during the late afternoon and early evening. You may catch sight of a larger bird amongst the flocks of Swallows and martins feeding overhead. With its dark plumage and swept-back wings, at first it may look like a giant Swift; but its flight action soon gives it away as a bird of prey. It is a Hobby, on the lookout for large insects or even a House Martin to satisfy its appetite. If you are really lucky, you will witness a kill, as the Hobby manoeuvres itself through the flock, twisting this way and that until it reaches out and grabs its target with sharp talons.

This elegant falcon was once very rare, breeding on heathlands in central southern Britain only, but its population has boomed in recent years, a rare success story at a time when so many bird species are in decline.

Above: *If you are really lucky you may see a Hobby dashing after its prey – in this case a House Martin.*

Right and below: *Before they migrate, Swallows often gather together on wires, sometimes with their close relatives House Martins. Watch as some birds continue to feed, launching themselves off the wire to seize insects in mid-air, while other birds preen themselves.*

to stop it from going bad. Although rare, outbreaks of food poisoning such as botulism do occur amongst birds, and garden feeding stations are the perfect place to breed disease.

You can minimize the risk of disease (and save some money into the bargain) by reducing the amount of food that you put out at this time of year. Between July and September, there is plenty of natural food available and long daylight hours in which to find it.

Rats and mice can also be a major problem at this time of year. Removing uneaten food, especially if it is lying on the ground, is one way to reduce the risk of pests.

Migration

Your garden may not seem the obvious place to observe migration, but you may be pleasantly surprised. By the end of the month, many species are beginning to move southwards and you may find birds such as the Whitethroat and Willow Warbler passing through.

A regular watch overhead, especially in the hour or so after dawn and before dusk, can produce some unexpected sightings. If nothing else, you will see growing numbers of Swallows and martins, boosted by the season's young birds. Swifts, however, have virtually disappeared from urban areas by the middle of August, gathering at sites such as reservoirs before heading south for the winter.

THINGS TO DO

- Look out for baby birds and watch their behaviour as they learn about their new world.
- Give your birdtable a regular clean to prevent disease.
- Look out for migrating birds which may stop off to feed in your garden.
- Keep putting out food for the birds; you will continue to get visitors to your birdtable and feeders.
- Top up water in your pond and birdbath.

September

After the uneventful late summer months, this first autumn month brings much greater changes to the birdlife of your garden. The first official month of autumn can vary dramatically weather-wise, with severe gales sometimes giving way to a minor heat-wave, even in the last week of the month. Keen gardeners would do well to be aware that, even in southern Britain, there could be an early frost.

Meanwhile, September is a month of comings and goings. The Swifts have already long gone and Swallows and House Martins will soon join them. As compensation, the first winter visitors may arrive, such as Fieldfares and Redwings, especially in gardens in the north or east of Britain.

Other birds that may increase in numbers include Jays, boosted by arrivals from the Continent. In some years, there may be a major influx of these colourful birds. Other members of the crow family, such as Jackdaws, form flocks at this time of year, and may either be seen overhead or come to visit your garden to feed.

During the month, you will need gradually to increase the amount and variety of food on offer, moving to high-energy foodstuffs, such as sunflower hearts, and putting out old fruit, such as apples and pears, for thrushes, including Blackbirds.

Time to go...

One of the most evocative sounds of September is the twittering of flocks of Swallows, Sand and House Martins as they gather on telegraph wires before, at some unseen signal, they head off to begin the long journey southwards to their winter grounds in Africa. Swallows have the longest journey of all: more than 5,000 miles (8,000 km), all the way to South Africa, where they will spend the southern summer in a land of plenty while we (and our resident species) suffer the cold, dark, northern winter. House Martins spend the winter less far south, but must still cross the whole of Europe, the Mediterranean Sea and the mighty Sahara Desert before reaching a place to spend the winter.

Above: *House Martins are one of the last summer migrants to depart. Like their close relatives the Swallows they usually gather on telegraph wires, twittering to each other before heading off to Africa.*

Left: *Meanwhile, resident species such as the Jay are fattening themselves up for the deprivations of the winter to come. This bird is gorging itself on berries.*

Migration may seem an incredibly hazardous lifestyle, but so is staying put. The chances of a Wren or Robin surviving the winter here at home are less than fifty-fifty, whereas the Swallow probably has a better than even chance of returning to breed the following spring.

Nevertheless, the hazards on migration are many and varied, and include predators, starvation, drought and, of course, the fickle weather. No wonder we watch these autumnal gatherings of hirundines (Swallows and martins) with mixed feelings, and miss the birds when the time finally comes for them to depart. It will be at least six months – and possibly longer – before we see them again over our gardens.

Above: *Autumn is a time when pond life is slowing down, but as a pond owner you need to work extra hard to keep the pond free of leaves.*

Spring-clean in autumn

Paradoxically, early autumn is the time to give your garden and its various bird attractions a thorough spring-clean. You should inspect your nestboxes and remove any debris such as nesting material and unhatched eggs or dead chicks (sometimes a fairly gruesome and unhygienic task, so wear rubber gloves). If necessary, take the box down and give it a thorough scrub with soapy water, then rinse and let it dry thoroughly before replacing it.

Autumn is also a good time to clear debris from your pond; and place a guard over the water surface to catch falling leaves, which otherwise will be a problem to clear up later. Check that the edges of the pond are not too overgrown and that the lining itself has not sprung a leak.

It is also time to begin pruning trees and shrubs, removing unnecessary foliage and ensuring vigorous, healthy growth during the following year. By looking after your garden you will get it in tip-top condition for the following spring, ready for the breeding birds. Keep some of the cut off branches in a pile – a perfect home for beetles and other invertebrates, which, in turn, are food for the birds.

THINGS TO DO

- If you haven't already, consider putting in a garden pond (see *Further Reading*). Now is the time to start planning the location, getting together all the equipment needed, and so on.
- Make a note of the last date when you see summer visitors such as House Martins and Swallows overhead.
- Look out for the first autumn visitors such as Jays, and flocks of Fieldfares and Redwings.
- Increase the levels of bird food that you supply in your feeders and on your birdtable.

October

This is the classic month of autumn, when the heat of summer finally gives way to the cool, frosty weather of the winter to come. From a bird's point of view, the test begins here: will they manage to find enough food to survive until the spring, or will they fail to do so and eventually starve to death or be eaten by a predator?

Like September and November, October is a month of movements: the last summer visitors such as House Martins finally leave our shores, while the main arrivals of

Above: *Goldcrests are a regular garden visitor in autumn, when they join together in small parties to search for insect food. The bird on the left is a juvenile, lacking the adult's distinctive yellow crest.*

winter visitors, including thrushes, Robins, Goldcrests and tits, really gets underway. Many of these tiny birds fly here from Scandinavia, to spend the winter in a much milder climate, where they have a better chance of surviving. By putting out food, our gardens are a welcome oasis for many of these small birds, especially as the nights draw in and temperatures begin to drop.

Weather-wise, October can be very varied: we can enjoy the balmy temperatures of a so-called Indian Summer, or suffer the devastating effects of an autumnal gale such as the Great Storm of October 1987, which wreaked so much havoc and destruction in southern Britain.

Tiny visitors

You are spending a quiet afternoon at work in the garden, sweeping up the autumn leaves into piles, when you become aware of a thin, high-pitched sound coming from somewhere above your head. Look up, and at first you may not see them, but watch out for a movement that gives away their presence. It is a flock of Long-tailed Tits, whose

Left: *Another regular autumn visitor to gardens is the Long-tailed Tit: a beautiful pink, brown and cream bird, which often allows very close views, as it is very tame and seemingly oblivious to humans.*

THINGS TO DO

- Now is the time to dig your pond (see box). This will give the plants that you decide to have plenty of time to become established before spring.
- On fine nights and early mornings listen out for migrants passing overhead.
- If you haven't already, clean out your nestboxes, removing any debris.
- Save some apples and other fruit for the winter, to feed blackbirds and winter thrushes.

DIG A POND

If you fancy a spot of hard work, why not build yourself a pond, before the ground gets too hard? October is an ideal month to create a garden pond, as the plants will have plenty of time to become established before the following spring.

Make sure you plan carefully, as there will be no opportunity to rectify major mistakes once you have got started. If in doubt, get advice from a friend or neighbour who has done it before.

contact calls have drawn your attention. Now you see them: tiny balls of buff, black and pink, with impossibly long tails stretching out behind them as they flit from twig to twig in search of tiny insects to eat.

Listen again, and there is an even higher-pitched note. This belongs to another tiny bird – indeed, Europe's smallest – the Goldcrest. Incredibly, this minuscule member of the warbler family actually spends the whole winter in Britain, surviving by embarking on a constant search for tiny invertebrates to eat.

Goldcrests often join in with flocks of tits, especially Long-tailed, in order for each individual to have a better chance of searching for food. If you stay quiet and still, both Long-tailed Tits and Goldcrests can be incredibly tame, coming almost close enough to touch before flitting off again, leaving you amazed at the intimacy of your encounter.

Robins singing

October is generally a fairly silent month, although one bird is an exception to the rule. Unlike most small birds, Robins do not join together in flocks for the autumn and winter, but continue to defend territories. For this reason, both males and females sing their beautiful song throughout the season.

Robins also often sing at night, stimulated to do so by the light from street lamps. For this reason, they are often mistaken for Nightingales by members of the public. Convincing someone that the songster in his or her garden is just a Robin rather than something more exotic can be a problem.

Below: *The only songbird to sing regularly during the autumn months is the common and familiar Robin, which holds territory all year round.*

November

November is a month of great change, brought on by two things: the decrease in day length, and a drop in temperatures. As a result, birds may struggle to find food in their natural surroundings, such as fields and woods, and look for alternatives. For many, especially those that live near human habitation, the best bet is to join together in flocks and head into villages, towns and cities: to our gardens.

So, November is a good month to be at home during daylight hours, especially soon after dawn or before dusk. If you do go out to work, it's still worth spending a few minutes at your kitchen window, looking out into your garden. You'll be amazed at what you sometimes see. Don't forget to keep your garden bird log up to date: not just a list of species, but numbers and details of behaviour too.

Tit flocks

Tit flocks are one of the most prominent of garden visitations in late autumn and winter. You may well have had a pair or two of Blue Tits or Great Tits nesting in your garden in spring and summer, and late summer often sees family parties of tits visiting gardens. It's not really until November, however, that the true feeding flocks arrive: as

Above: Various species of tits and other small birds often travel in flocks in autumn and winter, in order to maximize their chances of finding food. Listen out for their high-pitched contact calls as they try to stay together.

many as 20 or 30 birds, often made up of several species, including Coal, Marsh and Long-tailed Tits. The first sign is usually an aural one: a set of high-pitched squeaks, signalling the birds' arrival. Then you see them: hopping around the branches of trees and bushes, picking off tiny insects, before they head off again as quickly as they came, leaving only silence behind.

The calls are designed to help the birds keep in contact with each other. Unlike spring and summer, when birds pair up and hold territories, actively avoiding their rivals, autumn and winter are a time of co-operation. Joining together with other birds has two advantages: the group can share any food resource that is found by any of its members, and being in a large gang may provide some defence against predators, since several pairs of eyes are better than one and a predator confronted by a flock may be confused (and may not choose you!).

If a tit flock does visit your garden, make sure that you take a good look for 'hangers-on' such as Goldcrests,

Nuthatches and Treecreepers. If you're really lucky, you may even see a Lesser Spotted Woodpecker tagging along, or even a much rarer bird (several autumnal vagrants from far afield have survived the British winter by joining up with commoner species).

Above: *Redwings will visit your garden if the winter is fairly harsh. Keep water unfrozen and ensure a good food supply such as apples on your lawn and berry-bearing plants, on which all thrushes like to feed.*

Looking and listening

November is also an excellent time to add a few unexpected species to your 'garden list'. Flyover species count, so, just after dawn or before dusk, go out into your garden and listen out for the tell-tale calls of migrant birds passing high overhead. Redwings, Fieldfares and Skylarks are all regular at this time of year.

Much songbird migration takes place at night, so if you're really keen you may want to try a midnight vigil. Clear, frosty nights with a full moon are often the best, but make sure that you wrap up warm.

Evening is also a good time to watch birds going to roost. If you are on a flight-line, say between a park or woodland and a reservoir or flooded gravel-pit, you will see large flocks of gulls, ducks and geese flying overhead, usually in loose formation. Joining them may be crows, thrushes and finches, and many other species, all going off to find a safe place to spend the night.

THINGS TO DO

- Finish off all the necessary pruning and other garden chores.
- Begin to increase the supplies of food, especially energy rich seeds, and regularly refill feeders, as they tend to empty quicker and quicker at this time of year.
- Check your garden pond for fallen leaves, and clear them out if necessary.
- Don't tidy up unnecessarily; a fallen branch, a loose stone, a tangle of plants all provide habitats for other wildlife.
- Erect a birdtable if you don't already have one, in preparation for the harsh winter ahead. If you already have a birdtable, clean it thoroughly along with any birdfeeders.
- Keep the water in your birdbath from freezing.

December

The last month of the year is often one of the most eventful in the garden, with colder weather forcing many more birds to move in from surrounding habitats to search for food. Winter visitors, such as Redwings and Fieldfares, may be present in good numbers, while 'the usual suspects' – tits, Robins, Wrens, Starlings and House Sparrows – are likely to be regular visitors to your birdtable and feeders.

Remember that frosty nights mean that the usual sources of water for drinking and bathing may be frozen

over, so make a habit of refilling your birdbath with clean, warm water every morning, especially if you are off to work at an early hour.

And of course, as the weather gets colder, and the days draw in, don't forget to increase the amount of food, and regularly refill feeders, as they tend to empty quicker and quicker at this time of year.

Thrushes, berries and fruit

All the five common species of British thrush (Song Thrush, Mistle Thrush, Redwing, Fieldfare and Blackbird) are partial to fruits and berries, especially in winter when their usual diet of worms and grubs will be very hard to find.

You can help these birds in two ways. First, by planting berry-bearing bushes such as holly, hawthorn and cotoneaster. These will soon bear plenty of ripe, luscious fruit, just at the time when the birds need it most, in late autumn and winter. Mistle Thrushes will often defend a berry-bearing bush for several weeks or even months, fighting off all-comers until the fruit is all gone. Other members of the thrush family are more co-operative, feeding alongside members of their own and other species, so that mixed flocks of Redwings and Fieldfares are a common winter sight in some areas of the country.

The other, much quicker way to attract thrushes into your garden is to put out some old apples on the ground beneath your usual feeders. These will often attract hungry Blackbirds, which are very partial to soft fruit.

Christmas time

For many busy people, the Christmas period is one of the few occasions when they have plenty of time to

Left: *Blackbirds love feeding on windfall or rotten apples, which provide easy-to-obtain energy to keep them in good condition throughout the winter.*

WAXWINGS

If you are really lucky, you may even get a flock of Waxwings, the most sought-after (and arguably the most beautiful) of all our winter visitors. Waxwings exhibit irruptive behaviour, which means that numbers vary dramatically from year to year depending on the state of the berry crop in their native Scandinavia and Russia. In 'good' Waxwing years, several thousand may appear, generally on and around the East Coast, before spreading farther inland. They often appear in gardens, and may hang around a particular berry bush until all the fruit has been consumed.

If you do get a flock of Waxwings, be prepared for another invasion: that of dozens of birdwatchers peering into your garden to look at them.

Right: *The ultimate garden visitor is surely the Waxwing, a rare and occasional visitor from Scandinavia and northern Russia, which feeds mainly on berries.*

watch birds in their garden. So, if you do have a few days off during the festive season, take advantage of this in two ways. First, do all those little jobs that you have been putting off all year such as giving your birdtable and feeders a good scrub, or clearing out debris from nestboxes, so that the birds can breed again there the following spring. Secondly, take time to enjoy the fruits of all your hard work and spend an hour or two just sitting at your window watching the birds in your garden, and getting to understand their behaviour. And, when you finally finish the celebrations, don't forget that birds enjoy a bit of Christmas pudding as much as you do.

THINGS TO DO

- Wrap up warm one evening and count the birds passing overhead on their way to roost.
- Put out leftover food on your birdtable, especially in harsh weather. Increase the levels of other foods you put out too.
- Look over your notebook for the year, and relive happy memories of the birds you've seen in your garden.

Troubleshooting

This chapter might be entitled 'Garden Wars': as it covers all the things that you wish that you didn't have in your garden such as pests and predators, cats and squirrels, rats and mice, Magpies and slugs, and the dangers from pesticides. You may disagree with some of my suggestions, or even develop new ones for yourself (in which case I should be glad to hear from you). Good luck!

Pests and Predators

When you begin to attract birds into your garden by providing food, water and places to nest, you also make them vulnerable: to disease, and especially to predators. Your birdtable may be providing food for the birds, but to a cat or Sparrowhawk it also offers the avian equivalent of a free lunch.

You also have to deal with less obvious threats: squirrels, which steal food and birds' eggs; Jays and Magpies, which can wreak havoc on nesting birds; and, of course, pests such as rats and mice which will welcome a new supply of food. Not to mention those hidden pests: insects, slugs and snails, and aphids (see below).

Rats and mice

Rats and mice can be a problem, especially if they get into your home. To discourage them, make sure that you do not overfeed the birds so that there are left-overs at the end of the day; clean up regularly (especially underneath the birdtable and feeders); and make sure that you store seeds and nuts carefully in air-tight containers where the rodents can't get at them.

Left: A Sparrowhawk may be a surprise visitor to your garden, creating havoc with the feeding songbirds on your birdtable.

Above: Jays may catch nestlings from the nest.

Right: No-one wants to welcome troublemakers like Brown Rats into their garden: make sure you clean up waste food regularly.

If you have a serious problem with pests such as rats and mice, don't hesitate to call in the professionals to help you eradicate them from your home and garden. A speedy response is essential if you do not want the birds, or other wildlife, to suffer.

Squirrels

Everybody loves the native Red Squirrels, but there are now few parts of Britain where they occur. With the non-native Grey Squirrels, you either love them or hate them. Some people turn the presence of squirrels into an advantage: creating complex and bizarre obstacle courses to test the squirrels' ingenuity and provide hours of amusement. Other people try their best to turn their garden into a squirrel-free zone. The biggest problem may be their

Left: *Squirrels have ingenious ways of getting into supposedly squirrel-proof metal feeders in order to reach the peanuts inside!*

Below: *This Sparrowhawk has been successful and has caught an unfortunate Starling, which, after plucking it, it will take back to its hungry chicks.*

ability to destroy even the best-made bird-feeder in a matter of minutes, which can be annoying and very expensive. You can try 'squirrel-proof' birdfeeders, which work – sometimes! And you can thwart squirrels by putting ingenious barriers below your bird-table. But eventually these acrobatic creatures tend to get their own way. Grey Squirrels also eat birds' eggs and nestlings, searching for nests and eating the contents just as they would eat nuts.

Birds

Not surprisingly, birds are also preyed on by other birds: either those, such as the Sparrowhawk, that eat the full-grown birds, or those, such as the Jay and Magpie, that raid

nests for eggs and chicks. Even very welcome birds such as Great Spotted Woodpeckers do sometimes plunder nests and eat the young.

In many ways, this is part of the natural cycle and you shouldn't try to resist it. If you are squeamish, however, you can reduce the carnage in several ways. First, make sure that your bird-table, birdfeeders and nestboxes are away from handy perches that would allow bird predators to seize an unwary songbird. Secondly, pro-tect nestboxes and other nest sites by put-ting wire mesh around, leaving a narrow entrance for the parent birds to get in and out while excluding larger predators.

Incidentally, despite popular myth, it is the numbers of prey available that controls the popula-tion of natural predators, not the other way around. So, while Magpies, Jays and Sparrowhawks have enjoyed population booms in recent years, while many songbird species have declined, the two trends are not linked in any way. For the real blame for the decline of our garden birds, I believe that we can turn to two culprits: our agricultural policies, and the British love of the domestic cat.

Cats

Cats are, in many gardens, the biggest prob-lem of all. Partly because there are so many of them; partly because we artificially maintain their numbers by keeping them as pets; but mainly because they are such effi-cient killing machines. Frankly, unless we do something to help them, most small birds in gardens don't stand much chance against the number-one predator.

Somewhere around 7 million cats live in the UK, of which about one-third - between 2 and 3 million - live ferally. Together, they are responsible for the deaths of somewhere between 25 and 75 *million* songbirds every year. Most of these would die of other natural causes even without cats, since a

Above right: *Magpies often take songbirds, such as this House Sparrow, to feed on.*

Right: *Cats are a major problem for many gar-den owners, as their lack of natural predators, and their keen predatory skills, means they are able to kill many nestlings and adult birds.*

Above: *Species that nest in bushes and shrubs, such as this Blackbird, are especially vulnerable to predation by cats.*

ports of the birdtable and the areas above and below a nestbox, very efficiently keeping cats at bay.

Personally, I would welcome the introduction of a licensing scheme, with the legal condition that all pet cats must be clearly tagged with their owners' details and (except those kept for breeding) neutered. Following this, the feral cat population could be culled, dramatically reducing the number of cats at large.

Why take such drastic measures? Because domestic and feral cats have no natural predators to keep them in check, and the population of domestic cats is kept at an artificially high level since their owners feed them.

There – I've said it! Now, if anyone wants to take up the cudgel and start an Anti-Cat League, that's absolutely fine with me.

Other Hazards

As well as to pests and predators, birds may fall victim to a number of other hazards in your garden. These are not major hazards, but it is still distressing if you find that a bird has been killed or injured as a result of them, so they are worth attending to.

pair of most species of garden bird will rear several young and, for a stable population, only two (of the original pair and their offspring) need to survive to breed in the following year. It can, however, be very distressing for us to see our favourite birds being killed before our eyes.

But let's face it, cats are not going to disappear, so we do need to do something. But what? A bell on the cat's collar will help to even up the odds; and you can buy cat alarms that are supposed to discourage cats from entering your garden. If you own a cat, having it neutered will ensure that it doesn't add to the feral population. Providing nest-sites and feeding places that are out of reach of cats, or are protected from them, will also help considerably. Two of the best methods of protection are natural. A really prickly holly bush, gorse bush or barberry bush will not only provide safe nest-sites, but branches can also be 'harvested' and used to protect the sup-

Glass windows and doors

Birds cannot see panes of glass very easily and, especially if there is light behind the glass, or they can see their own reflections, they may attempt to fly straight through the pane of glass itself. Large birds, such as Sparrowhawks and pigeons, usually only stun themselves, but for smaller species, such as Robins, a collision usually brings a swift and sudden death.

From time to time, a male bird will also attack his own reflection, under the misapprehension that it is a rival male that has entered his territory. Although this rarely results in death or injury, it may waste valuable energy at a critical time of year: the breeding season.

So, to prevent collisions and other problems, you can fix a silhouette of a hawk (or indeed almost any obvious shape) on the inner surface of a window or door, which will deter most birds from flying straight into the glass.

Water

As well as being essential to their survival, water can also bring death to birds. Small birds in particular may drown if they fall into a water barrel or rainwater tub. Either cover the tub completely, or, if you want to collect rainwater, just put a wooden plank over the top of the tub so that the birds have somewhere to perch while drinking. A branched stick or twig jammed into a container will also help a struggling bird to extricate itself from the water.

Pesticides and herbicides

This is a difficult subject, as many people who wish to attract birds and other wildlife to their garden are also keen gardeners and do not want to see their precious plants nibbled by aphids, caterpillars, slugs, snails and other so-called 'pests'.

In fact, by encouraging birds into your garden at all you are halfway to winning the battle. A healthy population of birds will act as a natural pest-control system, keeping numbers of many invertebrates down by exploiting them as a food resource. This biological warfare clean-up squad does a very good job (particularly Blue Tits, which love caterpillars, and Song Thrushes, which will control your snail population). You should also encourage other predators such as hedgehogs (which love slugs), frogs and toads, and, of course, ladybirds, (which love aphids).

So, although it is tempting to use chemical warfare in the fight against insect pests, try to resist it. Using potent chemicals only masks the problem, and also runs the risk of poisoning the very birds that you love to see. Also garden

chemicals, though much safer than they used to be, may still pose risks to human health.

Failing this, you can always turn for advice to organic gardening experts, who have developed all sorts of ways to deal with the problems posed by insect pests without using harmful chemicals. See *Useful Addresses* for details.

Above: *This mark on a window shows where a large bird – probably a Sparrowhawk – hit the glass.*

Below left and right: *You don't need to use pesticides to prevent caterpillars and snails from eating your plants: just encourage Blue Tits and Song Thrushes instead!*

Identifying Birds in your Garden

This chapter is designed to help you identify the various species of bird that visit, or fly over, your garden on a regular or occasional basis. It is split into three parts: **Regular Species**, **Unusual Species** and **Flyover Species**.

The first, **Regular Species**, includes common and familiar birds such as the Blackbird and Robin, as well as more occasional but still regular garden visitors such as the Treecreeper and Spotted Flycatcher.

The second, **Unusual Species**, includes many less regular garden dwellers such as Lesser Spotted Woodpecker, Hawfinch and Redpoll, as well as some species common in continental Europe but rare or absent from British gardens such as White Stork, Hoopoe, Serin and Golden Oriole.

The final category, **Flyover Species**, is divided up into groups or families such as Raptors, Wildfowl and Gulls, and includes the many species that, though they rarely if ever actually visit gardens, may be seen flying overhead.

The accounts are designed to give you an insight into the bird itself, and are written largely from a personal point of view. If you want more detailed information, for example on specific identification features, then there are many excellent field guides available.

Remember that no garden will play host to all, or even the majority of these birds, so make sure you check identification carefully before claiming an unusual visitor. On the other hand, during my time spent living mainly in suburban west London I have recorded the following species either in or over ordinary gardens: Little Owl, Yellow Wagtail, Hobby, Osprey and Arctic Skua – so don't dismiss anything as impossible!

Left and above: *Grey Heron (left) and Kingfisher (above) are two species that may be attracted to your garden, especially if you have a pond.*

Right: *The Magpie may not be the most popular garden bird visitor, but if you take a close look you just have to admire his stunning glossy black-and-blue and white plumage.*

REGULAR SPECIES

Grey Heron *Ardea cinerea* 90–100cm, 36–40in

The largest bird ever likely to visit your garden, a heron can be an impressive sight, especially if it decides to land and try to steal fish from your pond. If so, you may wish to take action by putting trip-wires across the water surface to deter this hungry predator. Herons are more often seen flying overhead, when their broad wings, hunched neck and trailing legs are distinctive. They often utter a deep, croaking call as they fly.

Shy birds, herons are also very vulnerable to prolonged spells of ice and snow in winter, when they may starve to death. If desperate, they may visit gardens and even take food from birdtables.

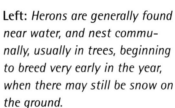

Left: Herons are generally found near water, and nest communally, usually in trees, beginning to breed very early in the year, when there may still be snow on the ground.

Above: Juveniles resemble the adults (left), but lack the distinctive black markings on the head.

Mallard *Anas platyrhynchos* 51–62cm, 20–24in

Britain's commonest and most familiar duck is the ancestor of most domestic ducks. Many people's first experience of birds is feeding the ducks and, if you live near a river, lake or pond, Mallards may even visit your garden to be fed.

Mallards breed early, and once the downy ducklings have hatched they are immediately able to forage for food. In spring, they often accompany their mother into gardens,

especially if food is provided regularly.

The male Mallard is very handsome and distinctive, with a bottle-green head and magenta breast. In contrast, the female may at first appear dull in comparison, but take a closer look and you will see the subtle markings and varied shades of brown, buff and black that make up her plumage.

Above: Mallards frequently fly over gardens, especially if you live near a river or lake.

Right: In mid-summer, Mallards go into a period of moult, known as 'eclipse' plumage, when males lose their bright colours and resemble the females.

Sparrowhawk *Accipiter nisus* 32cm, 12in

This shy raptor is commoner than you might think, though is most often seen as it dashes low through foliage in pursuit of its songbird prey. Alternatively, you may spot one as it soars high above the roofs of houses, circling while making alternate flaps and glides as it surveys the gardens below. Sparrowhawks declined dramatically after the Second World War, as a result of the widespread use of pesticides such as DDT. Fortunately, after the chemical was banned, the population underwent a boom, and this delightful raptor is now a regular visitor to gardens, especially those in well-wooded suburbs, towns and villages.

Above: *Watch out for the Sparrowhawk's characteristic low, rapid flight as it hunts.*

Right: *As its name suggests, this species feeds mainly on small birds such as sparrows and tits, which it seizes with its sharp talons.*

Above: *Like many birds of prey, the male Sparrowhawk is smaller than the female (right); he has a distinctive blue-grey back and pale underparts barred with orange.*

Kestrel *Falco tinnunculus* 32–36cm, 13–14in

Britain's commonest raptor is widespread in towns and cities, where it preys on small rodents and birds. Although it rarely breeds in gardens, it may often be seen soaring or gliding overhead.

Kestrels nest in holes in trees, and can sometimes be persuaded to use specially designed nestboxes which have an open front. They will also sometimes nest on buildings. They lay three to six eggs, which they incubate for four weeks. The young fledge after four or five weeks.

Their call is a high-pitched 'kee-kee-kee'.

Right: *Kestrels hover in their characteristic hunting pose searching for their prey. This habit gives the species its old name of the 'windhover'.*

Left: *Male Kestrels are slightly slimmer and smaller than females (far left), and have a blue-grey head, chestnut back and pale underparts marked with fine spots. Females are more uniform in appearance, with rich brown upperparts streaked with black, and streaked underparts.*

Pheasant *Phasianus colchicus* 52–90cm, 20–35in

Originally introduced to Britain from Asia, probably by the Romans, the Pheasant is by far our commonest gamebird. Many are artificially bred for shooting, so in some rural areas it may be very common indeed. Pheasants are often very tame, and, although their usual habitat is fields and woods, they will often venture into large gardens to feed, sometimes even using birdtables.

The plumage shows great variation, with occasional very dark individuals, and some with and others without a white collar.

Once the chicks hatch they are, like all gamebirds, capable of leaving the nest immediately, and may be seen following the female in search of morsels to eat.

Below right: *In contrast to the male (below left) the female is beautifully camouflaged so that she can sit tight on her eggs without being seen.*

Above: *The Pheasant's wings beat very rapidly in flight.*

Right: *The male Pheasant is one of the most handsome British birds, with his long tail, rich chestnut plumage and distinctive head pattern.*

Black-headed Gull *Larus ridibundus* 35–38cm, 14–15in

This species has adapted to life away from the sea better than any other gull, and is a familiar sight everywhere, especially in winter, when it forms large flocks. It is by far the commonest of the small gulls.

Black-headed Gulls often visit gardens, frequently squabbling over food and being quite aggressive to other garden birds. They may also be very noisy. Watch out for young ones, which have dark patterns on their wings.

Like many successful species, Black-headed Gulls will eat more or less anything on offer, especially kitchen scraps and stale bread, which they often snatch by swooping down and picking it up on the wing. They breed in large colonies, well away from gardens, so are often absent in the spring and summer months.

Right: *In flight, look out for the pointed wings of both adult (right) and first-winter (left).*

Right: *The name of this species is something of a misnomer: in breeding plumage (bottom), it sports a dark, chocolate-brown hood, while outside the breeding season this disappears to leave a small dark spot behind the eye.*

Far right: *In first-summer plumage the Black-headed Gull has dark markings on the head and wings.*

Feral Pigeon *Columba livia* 31–34cm, 12–13in

This is surely one of the most familiar yet most overlooked species of bird in Britain. Because of their dubious ancestry, we tend to ignore them, yet from a behavioural point of view they are fascinating, especially when indulging in their complex courtship display.

Feral or Domestic Pigeons are descended from the wild Rock Dove, a shy species now confined to remote coasts of Scotland and Ireland.

In some areas, Feral Pigeons have become a real pest,

as their tendency to form large flocks and raise multiple broods means that they soon come to dominate a garden feeding station. Nevertheless, they deserve a bit more respect from birdwatchers than they get, and can provide hours of interest if you watch them carefully.

Left and above: Through interbreeding, Feral Pigeons have developed a wide variety of different colours and patterns, and a flock may appear to be a motley bunch.

Stock Dove *Columba oenas* 32–34cm, 13in

Often overlooked, this shy relative of the Wood Pigeon is commoner than you might think. It is often present in well-wooded rural and suburban gardens, giving itself away by its distinctive two-syllable song.

Stock Doves look superficially like Wood Pigeons, but can be told apart by their smaller size, distinctive yellow bill, and lack of white on their wings. Another good field mark is the iridescent green sheen on the sides of the neck.

Like other pigeons and doves, they breed most of the year around, starting in February and going on well into the autumn. They may raise up to five broods in a year, with two young per brood.

Above: *Stock Doves have a distinctive display flight in early spring, in which pairs fly in circles clapping their wings together.*

Right: *Compared to Feral Pigeons, they are much more delicately plumaged, with subtle shades of magenta and blue-grey.*

Wood Pigeon *Columba palumbus* 40cm, 16in

By far the largest European pigeon, the Wood Pigeon is very common, being found in most gardens. It has recently adapted to life in cities, often competing for food with the Feral Pigeon. It is also found in rural and suburban gardens, and its distinctive five-note cooing song is one of the classic sounds of the British summer.

Wood Pigeons are prolific breeders, nesting all year around, and raising two broods in a normal year. They feed on a wide variety of seeds, and can often be seen underneath birdtables, picking up spilt food. In winter, they will also feed on berries, clambering clumsily around a bush in order to find the juiciest ones.

Left: *Young Wood Pigeons lack some adult markings, so can be confused with Stock Doves.*

Left: *The white wing markings are easily seen in flight.*

Above: *Wood Pigeons are pretty unmistakable, with grey-and-purplish plumage, a white patch on the neck, and, in flight, distinctive white marks across the wings.*

Collared Dove *Streptopelia decaocto* 31–33cm, 12–13in

Unknown in Britain until the early 1950s, this charming dove is now a familiar garden bird, especially in suburbs and villages, where there are plenty of trees and shrubs in which they can nest. From just a single pair in Norfolk, there are now almost a quarter of a million pairs breeding here.

The characteristic, repetitive, three-note call is now a very familiar sound. It can often be heard, since, like many pigeons and doves, this species breeds virtually throughout the year, laying two white eggs. Collared Doves are prolific breeders, raising as many as five broods in a single year.

Below: *Collared Doves are easily identified by their slim appearance, pinkish-buff plumage and the distinctive black neck-ring that gives the bird its name.*

Left: *They are sociable, often visiting the garden in pairs or small groups, to feed on or underneath birdtables and feeders.*

Right: *In flight, they appear paler than other pigeons.*

Tawny Owl *Strix aluco 37–39cm, 15in*

Many people have heard the Tawny Owl's hooting call, but very few ever get to see the bird itself, let alone achieve good views. Listen out for the distinctive 'kee-wick' call.

Tawny Owls are highly sedentary, staying put on their breeding territory all year around, even during freezing winters. They usually eat rodents such as mice and voles, but when food is scarce they will also take amphibians and small birds.

They nest in holes and are found in well-wooded rural and suburban gardens with mature trees for nesting. They lay two to five all-white eggs, which they incubate for four weeks. Tawny Owls are found throughout Britain, but are absent from Ireland.

Below: The species' secretive nocturnal habits mean that it is rarely seen in daylight, unless you are lucky enough to discover one at its roost.

Right: Young often leave the nest before fledging.

Swift *Apus apus 16–17cm, 6–7in*

This is an extraordinary bird! Imagine a young Swift leaving its nest high in a tower in an English village, flying all the way to Africa, then returning to breed the following year, without ever landing. This truly is the perfect flying machine, and could hardly have a more appropriate name.

One day they are absent, the next day screaming overhead as if delighted to be back. The screaming once earned them the nickname 'devil birds'.

Swifts return to Britain in early May and may not breed for up to a month if the weather is bad. They lay two or three white eggs. The time taken to incubate eggs and fledge young also varies, depending on good or bad weather. Then, in August, they disappear, leaving behind only a memory of their sight and sounds.

Below: For many people living in towns and cities, the Swift is far more a sign of spring and summer than the more rural Swallow.

Left: When Swifts land they cling to walls, although you are far more likely to see them zooming around in the sky.

Green Woodpecker *Picus viridis* 31–33cm, 12–13in

The laughing call of the Green Woodpecker, which gives the bird its country name of 'Yaffle', is often the first sign that this beautiful bird is a visitor to your garden. If you have a large lawn, you may get a sighting of this shy bird, the largest British member of its family.

Green Woodpeckers feed mainly on ants, picked up from the ground, but may also be seen in trees, where they only very occasionally drum. Like all woodpeckers, the Green Woodpecker nests in a hole, excavated using its powerful bill. It lays a clutch of five to seven white eggs.

Left: *If you have a large lawn, you may get a sighting of this shy bird, the largest British member of its family. This is a juvenile.*

Above: *Easily identified by its yellow-green plumage, red crown and characteristic stiff posture, the Green Woodpecker is a regular visitor to large, rural or suburban gardens throughout England and Wales. It is, however, rare in Scotland, and, like other woodpeckers, does not breed in Ireland.*

Great Spotted Woodpecker *Dendrocopos major* 22–23cm, 9in

Our commonest woodpecker, the Great Spotted is a regular visitor to gardens, especially those with large mature trees, or ones near areas of parkland or woodland. The first sign of the bird's presence is often a clear, loud 'chip' call, followed by the distinctive sight of the bird itself, either in undulating flight or perched upright on the side of a tree trunk.

If you hear a woodpecker drumming, it is most likely to be a Great Spotted. They do so to attract a mate and to proclaim their territory.

They feed mainly on insects, which they prise from the bark of trees with their bill.

Left: *In flight, the Great Spotted Woodpecker shows distinctive oval patches on its wings.*

Above and right: *Great Spotted Woodpeckers are easily distinguished from the much rarer Lesser Spotted by their size (roughly the same as a Starling), white patches on the wings, and red under the tail.*
They nest in holes in trees, which they excavate themselves using their powerful bill.

Swallow *Hirundo rustica* 19–22cm, 7.5–9in

Our best-loved summer visitor undertakes one of the most epic journeys of any bird, migrating to and from its breeding grounds in northern Europe and its winter quarters in Africa, a round trip of around 12,000 miles.

Above: *Like their cousins, the martins, Swallows hunt for flying insects on the wing, especially on fine summer evenings.*

Once they arrive back, Swallows are a familiar sight in rural areas, often nesting in barns, but are also found in larger gardens.

After breeding, Swallows often gather on telegraph wires in late summer and early autumn, in preparation for their long journey southwards. They generally depart in September and return again the following April.

Left: *The Swallow is easily told apart from House and Sand Martins, and the unrelated Swift, by its longer tail, blue upperparts contrasting with white underparts, and brick-red throat. In flight, it utters a variety of twittering calls.*

House Martin *Delichon urbica* 12.5cm, 5in

As its name suggests, the House Martin lives alongside human beings, making its nest under the eaves of houses and other buildings, a far cry from its original habitat of caves and cliffs.

House Martins are neat and compact, with blue-black upperparts, smart white underparts and a very distinctive white rump, which is obvious when seen in flight. They return to Britain from their African winter quarters in April, and soon get down to the task of building a nest: a laborious process using tiny balls of mud, which they collect from the edges of streams, ponds and puddles. They leave in September or early October.

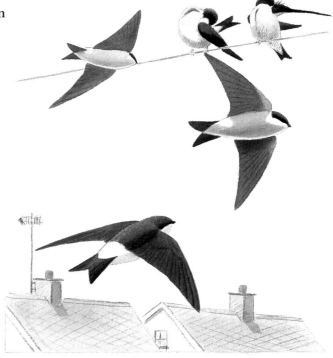

Left: *Where there is no mud available, you can help the species by providing artificial nestboxes.*

Above: *House Martins are found throughout Britain, and are a familiar summer sight in many towns and cities, though in recent years they have undergone a decline and may be absent from some former haunts.*

Pied Wagtail *Motacilla alba* 18cm, 7in

This handsome and elegant little bird is a familiar visitor to many gardens, often walking about on the lawn picking up tiny insects as it goes. Its two-note call is very distinctive.

In autumn and winter, Pied Wagtails can be sociable, especially at night, when they gather together in roosts of up to several hundred individuals. They nest in cracks or holes in walls, laying up to six eggs, which hatch after just

11 days or so. The young also fledge very quickly (sometimes after less than two weeks). This gives wagtails the opportunity to have a second or even third brood.

Left: *Its smart black-and-white plumage and long wagging tail make it easy to identify. Males are smarter, with more contrasting plumage than females.*

Above: *The race of the species that occurs in continental Europe (the White Wagtail,* M. a. alba, *above) is distinguished from its British and Irish counterpart (*M. a. yarrellii, *right) by its much paler back, contrasting with the black head and neck.*

Wren *Troglodytes troglodytes* 9–10cm, 3.5–4in

The tiny Wren is now our commonest bird, with more than ten million pairs breeding in Britain and Ireland. This is largely due to a succession of mild winters, which increase survival rates and help to create a population explosion.

As a result, this delightful little bird is now found in most gardens, In fact, you are more likely to hear the Wren than see it. Wrens feed by hopping about in rockeries and underneath trees and bushes, eating tiny insects. They build their nests in dense cover, usually near the ground, where they can raise their young away from predators.

Although highly territorial in summer, they become far more sociable in winter, often roosting with other Wrens in a nestbox.

Right: *For such a small bird, it has an incredibly loud song: a rapid series of notes ending in a flourishing trill.*

Left: *Wrens fly fast and low, their wings flapping in a blur.*

Left: *Its small size and furtive habits mean that it is not always easy to see.*

Dunnock *Prunella modularis* 14.5cm, 6in

Once known as the 'Hedge Sparrow', this member of the accentor family bears only a superficial resemblance to the familiar House Sparrow, and is more closely related to robins and chats. Dunnocks are shy and skulking, often being overlooked as they forage for food amongst the leaf litter beneath a shrubbery or at the base of a tree.

Dunnocks build their nest in dense undergrowth, partly to avoid being parasitized by Cuckoos. They lay four to six bright-blue eggs and raise two or three broods. They are most obvious in early spring, when the male sings his curiously uneventful song from a bush or tree.

Below: *At first, they may appear rather dull, but in fact they have a very subtly-marked and attractive plumage, and a very exciting sex-life. Watch out for a rival male trying to breed with another male's female, which is often guarded by her jealous mate to prevent any hanky-panky.*

Below: *Juvenile Dunnocks are even less colourful than their parents, with streaking on the head.*

Robin *Erithacus rubecula* 14cm, 5.5in

Britain's favourite bird is frequently featured on Christmas cards and is known for its tameness. Gardeners often find that they are joined by a friendly Robin as they dig. In fact, the bird is taking advantage of the newly turned soil to pick up earthworms and other grubs. Yet, over much of its original range in Europe, the Robin is a shy, woodland species that does not associate with man.

They are pugnacious and males will occasionally fight to the death in disputes over territory.

In winter, the British population is boosted by arrivals from the Continent.

Left: *Unlike many other song-birds, Robins sing all year round, as both males and females hold territory outside the breeding season.*

Left: *Juveniles are dull brown, spotted with buff.*

Right: *Male and female Robins both sport the distinctive orange-red breast that gave the bird its original name of 'Redbreast'.*

Blackbird *Turdus merula* 24–25cm, 9–10in

One of the most familiar and widespread of all our garden birds, the Blackbird is a firm favourite thanks to the male's attractive appearance, habits and beautiful song.

Blackbirds are early nesters, and often start to sing in late January or February, beginning to build their nests in March. They are amongst the most prolific of all garden breeders, raising up to five broods, each of three to five chicks.

To attract Blackbirds to your garden, plant plenty of climbers such as Clematis and Ivy, and in winter put out apples: Blackbirds love them.

Right: *A female Blackbird is much less conspicuous than her mate, lacking his yellow bill and sporting a brown plumage, suitable camouflage when sitting tight on eggs.*

Left: *Like other members of the thrush family, male Blackbirds often sing from a prominent post such as the top of a tree or the roof of a house.*

Fieldfare *Turdus pilaris* 25–26cm, 10in

This large and handsome thrush breeds in vast numbers in northern Europe, and several million come to spend the winter in Britain and Ireland, mostly foraging for food in the open countryside. In late winter, however, especially during spells of hard weather, they often visit gardens in search of food. Like other members of the thrush family, they are particularly partial to berries.

They generally arrive in October or November and depart north from March onwards, with only a few late stragglers in April.

Above: *Fieldfares often travel together in flocks, sometimes in association with the other winter visitor of the thrush family, the Redwing.*

Left: *The Fieldfare can be told apart from other thrushes by its large size (almost as big as a Mistle Thrush), and colourful plumage: grey head and rump contrasting with a russet back and warm buff underparts with black spots and a pale belly.*

Song Thrush *Turdus philomelos* 23cm, 9in

The Song Thrush is one of our best-loved and most popular birds, largely due to its memorable and tuneful song. They occasionally sing at night.

In recent years, Song Thrushes have undergone a mysterious and rapid decline, possibly as a result of food shortages due to the use of pesticides.

Right: *Its song is a distinctive repetition of notes and phrases, often delivered from a prominent perch such as the roof of a house.*

Below: *They feed mainly on worms and snails, which they smash on a stone to get at the contents.*

Song Thrushes are often confused with their larger relative the Mistle Thrush, but are in fact quite distinctive: smaller and neater, with rich brown upperparts and warmer buff underparts, with heart-shaped spots.

They build a neat, cup-shaped nest lined with mud and lay three to five sky-blue eggs faintly spotted with black. In winter, many head south to the Continent, to avoid food shortages caused by bad weather.

Redwing *Turdus iliacus* 21cm, 8in

They begin to arrive in October and November, but may not be seen in gardens until the New Year, when a spell of cold weather with snow and ice often forces them to seek alternative sources of food.

Given close views, the Redwing is very distinctive: smaller and darker than the Song Thrush, with a prominent buffish stripe above the eye, a densely streaked breast, and the warm orange-red patch on the flanks (not the wing!) that gives the species its name.

Redwings suffer badly from prolonged spells of harsh winter weather, so gardens are a real haven for them, especially if there are plenty of berry-bearing bushes. Like the Fieldfare, they head north to breed in March and April.

Below: *They are partial to fruit such as windfall apples and berries.*

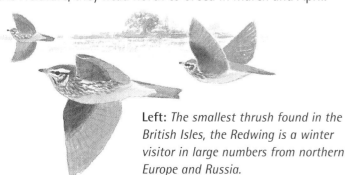

Left: *The smallest thrush found in the British Isles, the Redwing is a winter visitor in large numbers from northern Europe and Russia.*

113

Mistle Thrush *Turdus viscivorus* 27cm, 10.5in

This is the largest member of the thrush family found in Britain, being almost the size of a small dove. Mistle Thrushes are named because of a supposed preference for mistletoe berries, though in fact they will eat almost any suitable berry, especially in winter.

More commonly associated with large parks and areas of open woodland, Mistle Thrushes do nest in gardens, though they usually require large mature trees, and so tend to be more common in large rural gardens.

The song is distinctive, like a cross between the repeated phrases of the Song Thrush and the deep, fluty tones of the Blackbird.

Above: Like other members of its family, the Mistle Thrush is partial to worms.

Above: *The Mistle Thrush has a reputation for singing before and during thunderstorms, earning it the folk name of the 'Stormcock'.*

Above: *Mistle Thrushes can be told apart from Song Thrushes by their much larger size, paler general colour, less neat appearance and whitish tips to the outer tail feathers, and from Fieldfares by their much less colourful plumage.*

Garden Warbler *Sylvia borin* 14cm, 5.5in

One of the least familiar members of the warbler family, the Garden Warbler is in fact misnamed. Although it does occasionally occur in gardens (especially well-wooded, rural ones in southern Britain), it is more suited to areas of open woodland.

In fact, the Garden Warbler lacks any real identification feature and can be identified by its greyish-brown

plumage, large, beady eye, and larger size than Chiffchaff or Willow Warbler (from which it also differs by having no green in the plumage).

Garden Warblers arrive back in Britain in early May and depart south to Africa in late August, after breeding.

Above: *The Garden Warbler has an attractive song: like a speeded-up version of the Blackcap.*

Left: *It is a so-called 'sibling species' with the much commoner Blackcap, and can be easily distinguished, if you get a good view, by its completely plain head pattern, lacking the brown or black cap of its close relative.*

Blackcap *Sylvia atricapilla* 14cm, 5.5in

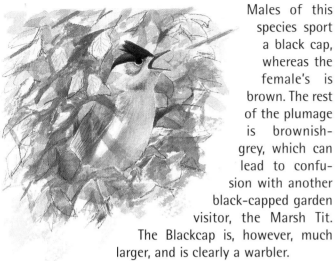

Males of this species sport a black cap, whereas the female's is brown. The rest of the plumage is brownish-grey, which can lead to confusion with another black-capped garden visitor, the Marsh Tit. The Blackcap is, however, much larger, and is clearly a warbler.

Blackcaps are a much more frequent visitor to gardens than they used to be, especially in autumn and winter. Those in winter are, however, quite different from our breeding population. They originate from central Europe and have only recently altered their migratory behaviour and route. Whereas once they spent the winter in Spain and North Africa, they now head westwards to Britain, where they find rich pickings in our gardens.

Left: Recently, Blackcaps have increased in numbers, and their rich, fluty song can be heard as early as late March or early April.

Above: This large and distinctive warbler is only partly well named: the males do sport a smart black cap, but the female's cap is chocolate brown.

Chiffchaff *Phylloscopus collybita* 11cm, 4–4.5in

The Chiffchaff is one of those birds, like the Cuckoo or Kittiwake, whose sound is so distinctive that it has given the bird its popular name. It is closely related to the Willow Warbler, which it resembles in appearance, but can easily be told apart is by their very distinctive songs.

Chiffchaffs have always been early arrivals to our shores and, after spending the winter in the Iberian Peninsula or North Africa, have traditionally returned in March.

Recently, some Chiffchaffs have begun to overwinter in Britain, especially in the south and west. If you have water in or near your garden you may well see one, as this attracts insects on which the birds feed.

Left: A member of the 'leaf-warblers', it most resembles its close relative the Willow Warbler, though has a somewhat darker and dingier plumage, and dark legs.

Right: In recent years, growing numbers of this delightful little warbler have spent the whole winter in the British Isles, often visiting gardens to find food.

Willow Warbler *Phylloscopus trochilus* 11.5cm, 4.5in

Many people are surprised to discover that this small, unobtrusive bird is in fact our commonest summer visitor, with more than two million pairs breeding here each year. It is not particularly common in gardens, preferring to nest on the edge of woods and heaths. If, however, you have a rural garden near one of these habitats it is well worth listening out for the Willow Warbler's distinctive song: a silvery cascade of notes accelerating down the scale, with a melancholy air.

Willow Warblers arrive back in Britain from mid-April onwards. After breeding, but before they head off to southern Africa for the winter, family parties of Willow Warblers may be seen foraging for food in gardens, the juveniles appearing much more yellow than their parents. The Willow Warbler forms a sibling pair with the Chiffchaff, but, although the two look very alike, their songs are completely different.

Left and above: *The Willow Warbler has one of the loveliest songs of all our summer visitors, full of beauty and melancholy. It often sings from the outer twigs of a bush or tree.*

Goldcrest *Regulus regulus* 9cm, 3.5in

At just 9 cm (3.5 inches) long it weights only five grams (one-fifth of an ounce). Yet, unlike many of their insect-eating relatives, which choose to migrate to avoid the British winter, Goldcrests manage to survive. They do so by gleaning tiny insects and other invertebrates from the bark and twigs of trees.

Above: *Goldcrests feed by hovering at the edge of the foliage and picking off tiny insects.*

Goldcrests are sociable little birds, and can be seen tagging along with other insectivorous species such as tits. They are often heard before they are seen, their very high-pitched call being distinctive once you have learned it.

In spring, Goldcrests build their nest in dense foliage, often in an evergreen bush or tree, and it may be quite hard to detect their presence until the adults begin coming to and fro to feed their young.

Left: *Once seen they are easily identified by the gold head stripe that gives the species its name.*

Right: *Along with its close relative the Firecrest, the Goldcrest is Britain's (and Europe's) smallest bird.*

116

Spotted Flycatcher *Muscicapa striata* 14cm, 5.5in

Spotted Flycatchers are one of the latest of all our summer migrants to return from Africa, often not arriving until the middle or even the end of May, and departing again in August or early September. They love sunny, rural gardens, especially those with old walls containing nooks and crannies where they can build their nests.

Like other sub-Saharan migrants, the Spotted Flycatcher is constantly vulnerable to changes in climate and may suffer badly if global warming leads to drought in Africa.

Left and below: This species is superficially warbler-like in appearance, with a brownish plumage, paler underparts covered with thin streaks, and the spotting on the crown, which gives the bird its name. They have a thin, dark bill and beady black eye.

Above: *The easiest way to identify them is by their habit of launching themselves off a perch to grab a flying insect in mid-air, then returning (usually to the same perch) to devour it.*

Long-tailed Tit *Aegithalos caudatus* 12–14cm, 5–5.5in

Although not related to the other tits, Long-tailed Tits also spend much of the autumn and winter travelling in loose flocks in search of food. They signal their arrival with a series of high pitched contact calls, then bounce from twig to twig, grabbing tiny insects as they go, before bounding away to another garden, their tails behind them.

Right: *Long-tailed Tits usually travel in flocks, often comprising family parties of birds.*

They lay up to a dozen tiny eggs, which hatch after two weeks or so. The young stay in the nest, which is almost always in a prickly bush, for another couple of weeks, but remain with the parents in a family group long after fledging.

In recent years, this species has benefited from a run of mild winters, so the population is booming.

Above: *This delightful and distinctive little bird is one of the firm favourites of any garden bird lover.*

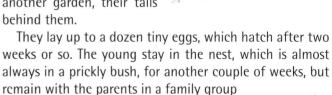

Right: *Long-tailed Tits also breed in some gardens, building an extraordinary barrel-shaped nest out of spider's webs, lichen and feathers: a real work of art.*

117

Marsh Tit *Parus palustris* 11.5cm, 4.5in

Once a regular visitor to gardens, especially those near damp wooded habitats, the Marsh Tit has undergone a decline in recent years and may be less regular than it once was. Nevertheless, it can still be seen in rural gardens, mainly in southern Britain and often comes to birdtables or peanut and seed feeders.

Until a hundred years or so ago, the Marsh Tit and its close relative the Willow Tit were considered to be the same species in Britain. March Tits are not yet found breeding in much of northern England or Scotland, but may take advantage of global warming to expand their range northwards.

Left and below: *They can be told apart from Willow Tits by the Marsh Tit's less bulky appearance, smaller head, glossier cap, and lack of a pale patch on the wing.*

Left: *Marsh Tits prefer to nest in holes in trees, often using an old woodpecker cavity.*

Left: *The Marsh Tit's plumage is at its most pristine in the early months of the year.*

Coal Tit *Parus ater* 11.5cm, 4.5in

Although it lacks the bright blues, yellows and greens of its commoner relatives, Blue and Great Tits, the Coal Tit does sport a smart, attractive plumage of brown, black, white and buff. It is a regular visitor to gardens, especially those near coniferous woodland where the species usually prefers to nest. Coal Tits often come to seed and peanut feeders, where they show great agility.

Coal Tits breed from April onwards, often nesting in a tree stump close to the ground. They lay up to nine eggs, which hatch about two weeks later, with the young fledging after two or three weeks. The species is single brooded.

Right: *Coal Tits have a distinctive white patch on the nape, easily seen when the bird is feeding.*

Left: *The juvenile Coal Tit is less bright and colourful than its parents.*

Left: *Coal Tits are superficially similar to Marsh and Willow Tits, but are smaller and more compact in build.*

Blue Tit *Parus caeruleus* 11.5cm, 4.5in

One of our best known and best loved garden birds, the Blue Tit is found in virtually every garden in the country. They usually prefer to feed on peanuts, cheekily nipping in to grab a morsel or two, while watching out for the ever-present danger from cats and Sparrowhawks.

Like other tits, they have white cheeks, and their underparts are yellow, with a hint of a dark stripe down the belly (though never so prominent as the Great Tit's). Along with the Coal Tit, they are the smallest in their family.

Below: Juvenile Blue Tits have yellow cheeks rather than the white cheeks of their parents.

Left: Blue Tits are highly flexible in their behaviour: they have learned to break into foil-topped milk bottles to get at the contents, and have adapted very well to using nestboxes.

Right: Blue Tits are easily told apart from their relatives, because they are the only species of tit to show any blue in the plumage: on the crown and nape, wings and tail.

Great Tit *Parus major* 13.5–14.5cm, 5.5–6in

The largest member of the tit family in Britain, the Great Tit is the size and weight of a House Sparrow.

Like its smaller relative the Blue Tit, the Great Tit is a frequent and regular visitor to most gardens, usually feeding on peanut or seed feeders. In spring, listen out for the distinctive two-note call, which sounds like 'tea-cher, tea-cher, tea-cher'.

Great Tits will readily take to nestboxes, though make sure that the entrance hole is large enough (at least 28 mm in diameter). Great Tits lay up to eleven eggs, which they incubate for 11–15 days. The young are fed mainly on caterpillars, and fledge after three weeks.

Below: Adult Great Tits are easily identified by their combination of smart black cap and throat, yellow underparts bisected by a thick black stripe down the belly, white cheeks, and olive-green upperparts and tail.

Left: Juvenile Great Tits have yellow cheeks and a less prominent black stripe down the belly than their parents.

Nuthatch *Sitta europaea* 14cm, 5.5in

The Nuthatch is unique: it is the only British bird that can climb *down* tree-trunks as well as up them. So watch out for the distinctive sight of a foraging Nuthatch, especially if you live near mature woodland or have large trees in your garden. The species will also come to peanut feeders, especially during spells of harsh winter weather, when natural food may be scarce.

In autumn, Nuthatches often hoard food such as acorns in preparation for the coming winter.

Nuthatches are quite common in rural England, but absent from Ireland and most of Scotland. As a result of global warming, however, they may begin to expand their range northward.

Right: *Given good views, the Nuthatch cannot be confused with any other species. It has steel-blue upperparts, rich orange-buff underparts, a paler throat, and a black 'bandit mask' through the eye. The bill is long and powerful, to prise out insects and nuts.*

Left: *In flight, the Nuthatch resembles a small, short-tailed woodpecker.*

Treecreeper *Certhia familiaris* 12.5cm, 5in

The Treecreeper is easy to overlook, but once seen, is unmistakable: no other bird creeps around the trunks and branches of trees in quite the same mouse-like manner. Treecreepers are very sedentary, but will move short distances from woods into gardens during spells of bad weather.

Surprisingly for such a shy bird, Treecreepers can be persuaded to use artificial nestboxes, designed to mimic the crevices in the bark of a tree-trunk where they would normally nest. They lay five or six white eggs spotted with brown, which they incubate for roughly two weeks.

Unlike the Nuthatch, the Treecreeper is found throughout Britain and Ireland, though is a less frequent visitor to gardens. In the Channel Islands, the common Treecreeper is replaced by the Short-toed Treecreeper *C. brachydactyla*.

Left: *They find their food by gleaning tiny insects from branches and twigs, which they prise out using their sharp, thin, decurved bill.*

Above: *The young are fed on tiny insects, and fledge after another two weeks or so.*

Jay *Garrulus glandarius* 34cm, 13in

Above: *In flight, look out for the Jay's distinctive white rump.*

Surely the most handsome British bird to visit gardens regularly, the Jay is both adaptable and intelligent – like other members of the crow family. It takes eggs and chicks from the nests of small birds, so, like the Magpie, is often unfairly blamed for population declines of songbirds. It has a crest, which it raises in courtship or anger, a delicate blue patch on the wing, and a prominent white rump, which is especially noticeable when the bird flies away.

Like most crows, Jays are omnivorous, though their staple diet in winter is acorns, which they harvest during the autumn and store for future use. In autumn, the number of Jays in Britain is augmented by an influx of immigrants from continental Europe. Jays occur throughout England and Wales, but are not found in northern Scotland and are rare in Ireland.

Right: *Given good views, the Jay is easy to identify, although in different lights its plumage can appear any shade from bright pink to brown.*

Magpie *Pica pica* 44–48cm, 17–19in

Depending on your point of view, the Magpie is either a ruthless predator responsible for destroying songbird populations, or a much-misunderstood and highly attractive bird.

Below: *With its black-and-white finery and long tail, the Magpie is unmistakable.*

In fact the recent meteoric rise in the Magpie population and decline of some of our most familiar songbirds is purely a coincidence, and Magpies cannot be blamed for the songbirds' problems, which stem mainly from changes in farming.

It is a common garden bird throughout most of Britain (apart from the far north and west) and is often seen in quite large flocks, the source of the famous rhyme recited by children. It is an opportunistic feeder, taking kitchen scraps and insects as well as chicks and eggs.

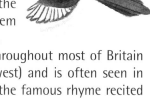

Above: *Many people admire the Magpie's undoubted beauty, but condemn its habit of preying on songbird eggs and chicks.*

Right: *Magpies are sociable birds, usually seen in pairs or larger groups.*

Jackdaw *Corvus monedula* 33cm, 13in

The smallest member of the crow family in Britain, the Jackdaw is also surely the most charming. It is usually associated with country villages, but in recent years has moved into many suburbs and small towns, where it finds rich pickings. In flight, it appears much smaller and shorter winged than its larger relatives, and can often be seen in pairs or small flocks, uttering the distinctive 'chack' call that gives the species its name.

They lay four to six eggs, which hatch two or three weeks later. The young leave the nest after four or five weeks. Jackdaws are single brooded.

Above: *Jackdaws usually nest in colonies, building their nests in holes in a wall, using sticks collected from nearby.*

Left: *The Jackdaw is easily told apart from the Rook and Carrion Crow by its much smaller size, short, stubby bill, and distinctive greyish patch on the back of its head.*

Rook *Corvus frugilegus* 47cm, 18.5in

The most rural of our common species of crow, the Rook is familiar in the country, being fond of arable farmland.

Except in rural areas, Rooks are not regular visitors to gardens, but may often be seen flying over, uttering their distinctive call.

They build an untidy nest out of sticks and lay three to six pale bluish eggs spotted with brown. The young hatch just over two weeks later and fledge four or five weeks after hatching. In autumn, watch out for Rooks 'tumbling' overhead in play, reputed to be a sure sign of bad weather on the way.

Below: *It can be told apart from the Carrion Crow by its smaller head, longer, more pointed beak, and greyish-white face patch.*

Left: *Rooks are very early breeders, nesting in large colonies known as rookeries.*

Right: *In flight, it appears longer winged and less bulky than the Carrion Crow.*

Carrion/Hooded Crow *Corvus corone* 47cm, 18.5in

Our commonest and most familiar large crow comes in two different races: Hooded Crow (*C. c. cornix*), confined to northwest Scotland (the highlands and islands) and Ireland, with a few in Anglesey in North Wales; and the more familiar Carrion Crow (*C. c. corone*), found throughout the rest of Britain.

Below: *The Carrion Crow is the only completely black bird (including bill and legs) in Britain. It is large, with a stout beak and broad wings.*

Both races are regular visitors to gardens, as they are opportunistic feeders and will eat almost any food you put out for birds. Their huge size means that they often dominate gatherings of other species, seizing the best morsels of food for themselves. They usually nest in trees, constructing an untidy nest out of twigs.

Above: *In flight, Carrion Crows appear broad-winged and bulky compared to Rooks.*

Right: *The Hooded Crow is very different in appearance, with large areas of grey on its back and underparts, contrasting with its black head, wings and tail.*

Starling *Sturnus vulgaris* 21cm, 8in

One of our commonest and most familiar garden birds, the Starling is often ignored in favour of superficially more attractive birds such as the Robin or Blackbird. Take a closer look, however, and you will be amazed.

Starlings have an extraordinary capacity for mimicry, so if you hear a mobile phone or car alarm going off check it out carefully: it may be that Starling perched on your roof. The usual song includes whistles, clicks and other noises that sound more mechanical than anything usually uttered by a bird. In winter, the British Starling population is boosted by arrivals from the east, many of which visit gardens.

Left: *In late summer, look out for the browner juveniles, which lack the glossy sheen and spots of their parents.*

Above: *Starlings have fascinating social habits, especially when feeding in flocks.*

Above: *Starlings have an intricately-marked plumage: glossy purplish-black spotted with paler markings.*

House Sparrow *Passer domesticus* 15cm, 6in

The House Sparrow is surely the most familiar yet one of the most overlooked garden birds; at least, it was until recently. Then, for reasons that we do not entirely understand, they began to decline in many areas, even disappearing from some gardens. The problem is worst in large cities like London, where sparrows are now virtually a rarity, but the decline has also occurred in rural areas.

Male House Sparrows are handsome birds, though females are the classic 'little brown job', lacking the male's dark bib and head markings. The species is highly sociable, often nesting together. So, if you still have House Sparrows in your garden, why not encourage them by putting up three or four nestboxes close together, so that the birds can form a small colony?

Above: *The juvenile House Sparrow resembles the female.*

Above: *The male House Sparrow is a much smarter bird than the dowdy female.*

Chaffinch *Fringilla coelebs* 15.5cm, 6in

Perhaps surprisingly to many people, the Chaffinch is one of the two or three most common birds in Britain. It is also a fairly regular visitor to many gardens, either feeding on open lawns, or, more recently, learning to take seeds and nuts from artificial feeders. With recent changes in farming practices meaning a reduction in available food, gardens are becoming more and more important for this species.

Chaffinches often breed in gardens, building their nest in the fork of a tree and laying three to five pale-blue eggs. They incubate for 11 to 13 days, and the young fledge two weeks later.

Right: *The male Chaffinch is very handsome and distinctive, with pink breast, prominent white wingbars, and a greenish rump.*

Left: *The female is less colourful, but can easily be told apart from the female House Sparrow by her white wingbars and sharp, pointed beak.*

Above: *In flight, both male (left) and female (right) Chaffinches show plenty of white on the wings.*

Greenfinch *Carduelis chloris* 15cm, 6in

As well as feeding on seeds and peanuts, Greenfinches also like to breed in gardens, often making their nest in the dense foliage of an evergreen tree such as a cypress, where it can be safe from predators.

Greenfinches breed from April onwards, laying three to six eggs, which hatch two weeks later. The young fledge two weeks after hatching, and can often be seen accompanying their parents to feed on seed and peanut feeders for several weeks afterwards. Greenfinches have two, sometimes even three, broods.

Left: *The Greenfinch is probably more dependent on food provided by human beings than any other member of its family, and can be found in gardens throughout the British Isles.*

Above: *The adult Greenfinch is easy to identify: no other bird has a plain, unstreaked green plumage and yellow on the wing. Females are slightly less bright, while juveniles can appear quite brown and streaky and may be confused with House Sparrows or Siskins.*

Goldfinch *Carduelis carduelis* 14cm, 5.5in

This delightful little finch is one of our favourite garden birds, though its visits may be few and far between.

Adult Goldfinches are pretty unmistakable: no other bird has their combination of red face,

black crown, wings and tail, and bright yellow flashes seen in flight. Their tinkling call is also very distinctive. Juveniles lack the red face of the adult.

In winter, many British-bred Goldfinches head south and west to continental Europe where the winter climate is milder, enabling them to find food. Their place may be taken by others from farther north and east.

Goldfinches build a delicate nest from grass, in the twigs of trees such as apple. They lay four to six eggs and have two or three broods.

Left: *Grow plenty of teasels, which in autumn produce tall seed heads that Goldfinches love to feed on, using their specially adapted sharp beaks to prise out the seeds.*

Siskin *Carduelis spinus* 12cm, 4.5in

Once a rare visitor to gardens, this tiny little finch has now become a familiar garden bird for many people, especially in rural areas near large patches of woodland. The population boom occurred because of the spread of coniferous forest plantations, where most Siskins breed.

Siskins often turn up in quite large flocks during the late winter months (February and March), when food shortages in the surrounding countryside force them to seek alternative supplies. In April, they head back north to breed, some birds travelling to Scotland or even Scandinavia.

Left: *Male Siskins can be told apart from their larger relative the Greenfinch by their smart black cap and bib, and black on the wings.*

Left: *They love peanuts, especially in red feeders, which may remind them of their natural food of alder cones.*

Right: *females and young are streakier in appearance. They also have a forked tail.*

Bullfinch *Pyrrhula pyrrhula* 16cm, 6.5in

Once a fairly regular visitor to many gardens, especially in rural southern Britain, the Bullfinch has sadly become very scarce in recent years, probably due to reductions in the supplies of natural food. Because it is shy, it has not readily adapted to artificial feeders like many of its relatives in the finch family.

Bullfinches breed from May onwards, laying three to six pale blue, black-spotted eggs, which they incubate for 12–14 days. The young then fledge just over two weeks later. Bullfinches feed mainly on seeds, which they crush in that huge bill; but in spring and summer they take the blossom from fruit trees, making them very unpopular with fruit farmers.

Left: *A male Bullfinch is unmistakable, with his bright, cherry-red underparts, black head and face, and huge bill. Females look like males, but have brownish underparts.*

Left: *In flight, Bullfinches show a distinctive white rump.*

UNUSUAL SPECIES

White Stork *Ciconia ciconia* 110cm, 40in

Long celebrated as a bringer of babies, White Storks are a familiar sight in villages and towns from Spain to Poland, though the species is not found in Britain or Ireland.

Having a stork nesting on your home is considered good luck in many countries, so people commonly build special platforms on the roofs of their houses or barns; or simply place an old cartwheel where the bird may choose to nest. Once a site has been chosen, storks are very faithful and will return year after year to nest.

White Storks winter in Africa, and arrive back on their European breeding grounds in April. They lay four large white eggs, which they incubate for four or five weeks.

Above: *The White Stork is one of the largest of Europe's breeding birds. Storks feed on a wide range of prey, especially frogs and rodents, which they seize with their powerful bills.*

Red-legged Partridge *Alectoris rufa* 34cm, 13.5in

Also known as the 'French Partridge', this attractive game-bird was introduced to southern Britain during the nine-teenth century, supposedly because it was hardier than its 'English' relative (the Grey or Common Partridge).

It is often bred for shooting and, as a result, can be quite common locally. Although far from a typical garden bird, it does regularly wander into gardens in rural areas, especial-ly those with long grass where it can find cover.

Like other gamebirds, Red-legged Partridges lay large clutches of eggs (up to 16 at a time), which they incubate for three or four weeks. The young can walk almost as soon as they hatch, and can fly after three weeks. They are fully grown after 16 weeks.

Right: *The Red-legged Partridge is easily told apart from its native relative by the striking face-pattern, striped flanks and, of course, its bright red legs.*

Moorhen *Gallinula chloropus* 31–35cm, 12–14in

A member of the rail family, the Moorhen (and its close rel-ative the Coot) have taken to water more than their rela-tives, evolving a lifestyle similar to that of dabbling ducks. Juveniles are less colourful and browner in appearance.

Moorhens often graze on open areas of grass, so are a localized but regular visitor to large gardens with open lawns, especially those near lakes, ponds or rivers where they nest. They build a floating nest, and lay 5–11 eggs. The chicks can swim as soon almost as soon as they hatch, though they are still very vulnerable to predators, espe-cially Pike.

The name Moorhen is in fact a corruption of the word 'Merehen': mere, meaning small lake, and hen, referring to any hen-like bird.

Above: *Adult Moorhens are easily identified by their brown and purplish plumage, jagged white line running along their flanks, and the colourful red-and-yellow bill.*

127

Turtle Dove *Streptopelia turtur* 26–28cm, 10–11in

The soft, purring call of the Turtle Dove was once the quintessential sound of the English summer; but sadly, in recent years, the population has suffered a major decline. This is largely due to persecution by marksmen with shotguns in southern Europe, who bag the birds as they pass through the Mediterranean region on their way south to spend the winter in Africa.

Turtle Doves can still be heard from May to August in rural parts of southern and eastern Britain, and occasionally visit gardens. Europe's smallest dove, they can be shy and elusive. They usually nest in a bush, laying one or two eggs, which they incubate for two weeks. Turtle Doves are prolific breeders, raising up to three broods in a single, brief breeding season.

Above: *Beware confusion with the superficially similar Collared Dove, which is much larger and less elegant, and lacks the subtle markings of the Turtle Dove.*

Rose-ringed Parakeet *Psittacula krameri* 38–42cm, 15–17in

This colourful, exotic member of the parrot family surely has no business being out in the wild in Britain. Yet it is! During the late 1960s and 1970s, escaped cagebirds established several feral populations in parts of the London suburbs. Despite hard winters, the birds thrived, partly thanks to people putting out food for them and other birds.

Today, at least 5,000 parakeets live in West London, with smaller populations elsewhere. Rose-ringed (or, as they are sometimes called, Ring-necked) Parakeets are now an established part of our fauna. They may possibly compete with other hole-nesting birds such as Starlings, Stock Doves and Jackdaws, but for many people they are a welcome addition to our avifauna.

Above: *They are noisy, sociable and impossible to miss. They signal their presence by a high-pitched screech as they fly overhead or perch in a tree.*

Right: *Once seen, they are unmistakable: bright lime-green, with short, narrow wings and a long tail.*

Cuckoo *Cuculus canorus* 32–34cm, 13in

The song of the Cuckoo must surely be the best known of that of any summer migrant to Britain and Europe; yet the bird itself is rarely seen, and for good reason. Cuckoos hide away to avoid the unwelcome attentions of smaller birds, which are threatened by the Cuckoo's habit of laying its eggs in other birds' nests.

They occasionally visit gardens, especially in rural areas, where they may parasitize Dunnocks.

They lay up to 25 eggs, depositing a single one in each nest and always sticking to the same host species. The egg hatches very quickly, after as little as 11 days, giving the young Cuckoo the chance to eject the host's eggs and chicks from the nest. The unsuspecting parent birds then feed this intruder, which fledges some two or three weeks later.

Right: *Cuckoos arrive back in Britain from their African wintering grounds in late April or early May and are most easily seen at that time of year.*

Barn Owl *Tyto alba* 33–39cm, 13–15in

Unlike the Tawny Owl, Barn Owls are much more likely to be seen flying during the day, especially at dawn and dusk, when they do much of their hunting for voles and other small rodents.

They are not exactly a 'garden bird', but in rural areas they may often venture close to larger gardens, and, as their name suggests, they are often associated with farming, especially during the breeding season. If you have a large garden near where Barn Owls occur, it may be worth considering putting up a nestbox designed especially to attract this beautiful bird.

They lay four to seven eggs, which they incubate for four or five weeks, the young fledging two or three months later, depending on the availability of food.

Right: *Barn Owls are easily identified because of their very pale, almost ghost-like, appearance, heart-shaped face and habit of flying low over open ground in search of their prey.*

Little Owl *Athene noctua* 21–23cm, 8–9in

This delightful bird, the smallest British owl, is in fact not a native species at all. Some were introduced from southern Europe over a century ago and gradually spread their range, which now covers most of rural southern and eastern Britain.

Little Owls prefer open country such as ornamental parks and traditional farmland, especially where there are hedgerows and mature trees

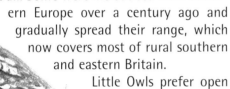

such as oaks. They feed on a wide variety of small prey, mostly earthworms, beetles and other invertebrates.

The species usually nests in a hole in a wall or more commonly a tree. They lay three to five white eggs, which hatch after three or four weeks. The young leave the nest early, after just a few days, but do not fledge for another three weeks or more, meanwhile being fed by their parents.

Left: *They occasionally wander and may be seen in both rural and some suburban gardens from time to time, especially in late summer after the young have fledged.*

Kingfisher *Alcedo atthis* 16–17cm, 6in

If you have a garden pond, and are very lucky indeed, you may receive a visit from Britain's most colourful bird, the Kingfisher. You hardly need a field guide to identify this species: apart from the dazzling blue upperparts, they have bright orange underparts, and a white throat. What surprises some people is their small size: at 16–17 cm (6–7 inches) only a little larger than a sparrow.

Unless you have a river or stream at the back of your garden, you will be unable to enjoy the spectacle of breeding Kingfishers. They nest in soft sandbanks, laying five to seven white eggs. They often have two, sometimes even three, broods. Listen out for their call, which often gives away their presence: a quiet, shrill, high-pitched and far-carrying 'chee'.

Above and right: *Be on your guard, you may see only a sudden flash of blue, and the bird is already gone; Kingfishers are quick hunters!*

Hoopoe *Upupa epops* 26–28cm, 10–11in

In mainland Europe, the Hoopoe is a familiar bird, especially where traditional farming methods allow lots of insects to survive. It is often given away by its distinctive and far-carrying call: 'hoo-hoo-hoo'.

In Britain, the Hoopoe is still a rare visitor, usually in April or May, when they occasionally turn up in southern parts of Britain, especially during warm spring weather with southerly winds. These birds have 'overshot' their intended destination as they return from wintering in Africa. Occasionally, a pair may arrive together and may even settle down to breed, nesting in a hole in a tree.

If global warming continues to bring a warmer climate to western Europe, the Hoopoe may begin to extend its range northward, possibly even crossing the Channel to become a regular British breeding bird.

Left: *Despite its bright orange-pink plumage, black-and-white wings and showy crest, the Hoopoe is shy and not easily seen.*

Wryneck *Jynx torquilla* 16–17cm, 6–6.5in

This unusual and distinctive relative of the true woodpeckers looks like no other bird. In addition it has the peculiar habit of twisting its neck from side to side in the manner of a lizard or snake.

In recent years, the Wryneck has suffered an unexplained decline, possibly due to food shortages, especially in the northern and western part of its range. As a result, it no longer breeds in Britain, where it was once fairly common.

The Wryneck can still be found in continental Europe, and, as a woodland species, has adapted to breeding in large, mature gardens and orchards, even using nestboxes when they are available. Like many hole nesters, it lays white eggs; it raises up to three broods.

Left and below: *It has a very peculiar plumage, with delicate grey, black and brown markings perfect for camouflage as it moves around tree trunks and branches in search of its insect food.*

Lesser Spotted Woodpecker *Dendrocopos minor* 14–15cm, 6in

The smallest European woodpecker, this little bird is also one of the shyest. It is most visible in winter or early spring, when there are fewer leaves on the trees, and it may be seen creeping along a branch like a Nuthatch. In winter, this species occasionally joins up with mixed feeding flocks of tits and other species.

You are most likely to have this species in your garden if you live in a rural area near broad-leaved woodland, and have large, mature trees where the birds can feed and nest. Listen out for soft drumming and a soft, high-pitched 'kee-kee-kee' call, but be patient: actually seeing this bird is rarely an easy thing to do.

Left: *This is a shy bird, rarely seen in flight.*

Right: *Lesser Spotted Woodpecker is easily told apart from its larger relatives Great Spotted (and in Europe Middle Spotted) by its much smaller size and barred white feathering on the back, lacking Great Spotted's large white patches.*

Yellow/Blue-headed Wagtail *Motacilla flava* 17cm, 6.5in

Scientists are fascinated by the genetics of this attractive little bird, which comes in more distinct races than almost any other, mainly told apart by their head pattern. Two races breed in northwest Europe: the Yellow Wagtail (*M. f. flavissima*), found in Britain, and the Blue-headed Wagtail (*M. f. flava*), in nearby mainland Europe.

Both are elegant, with olive-green upperparts and bright crocus-yellow underparts, though the juveniles are much duller. Both are summer visitors, wintering in sub-Saharan Africa and returning in April or early May. They breed mainly away from gardens and are most likely to be seen in spring, or in late summer and early autumn, when the young disperse after fledging.

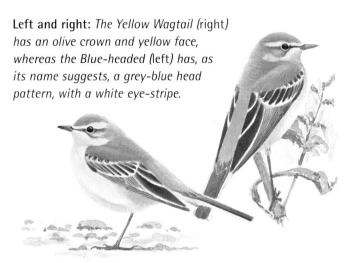

Left and right: *The Yellow Wagtail (right) has an olive crown and yellow face, whereas the Blue-headed (left) has, as its name suggests, a grey-blue head pattern, with a white eye-stripe.*

Grey Wagtail *Motacilla cinerea* 18cm, 7in

Of the three common European species of wagtail, this is the one most likely to be found near water. Grey Wagtails love fast-flowing streams and rivers, but occasionally wander, especially in winter, when they may be seen in rural gardens. They are also more likely to be seen in upland regions of the country.

It has an even longer tail than other wagtails and, when feeding, constantly bobs up and down, wagging its tail in a way typical of all its family.

Grey Wagtails usually nest in cracks in stone walls or bridges, often by rivers, streams or ponds. They lay four to six eggs, which hatch very quickly, after as little as 11 days. The young fledge two weeks later, giving time for two or three broods.

Above: *Despite its rather dull name, this is a beautiful bird, with soft grey crown and upperparts, black wings with white edges to the feathers, and varying amounts of white and lemon yellow beneath.*

Waxwing *Bombycilla garrulus* 17–18cm, 6.5–7in

If you live near the east coast of England or Scotland, and have plenty of berry-bearing bushes and shrubs in your garden, then watch out for Waxwings. They come from Scandinavia and northern Russia and their arrival usually coincides with food shortages there.

Given good views, Waxwings are very easy to identify: they have a pinkish brown plumage, feathery crest, and yellow and red on the wings, the red looking like drops of sealing wax, from which the species gets its name.

Waxwings usually arrive in flocks, but, as winter goes on, they may disperse into pairs and occasionally singletons. They feed voraciously on berries, for example Ivy and Cotoneaster, but on a mild winter's day they may be seen sallying forth for insects in the manner of a flycatcher.

Below: *Every few years or so, hundreds, sometimes even thousands, of these stunning birds 'erupt' westwards in late autumn, in search of berries.*

Nightingale *Luscinia megarhynchos* 16cm, 6in

Right: *Nightingales have a brown-and-buff plumage with a more rufous tail.*

This legendary songster is a summer visitor to Britain and Europe, arriving in late April or early May, when the males are likely to be in full song by day as well as, more traditionally, by night. They are secretive, preferring to stay deep in the cover of scrub or bushes, and so are heard far more often than they are ever seen.

If you do catch a glimpse of one, it is nothing to write home about. A Nightingale is a little larger than a Robin.

Nightingales are not normally found in gardens, though on the mainland of Europe, where they are more common than in Britain, they may occasionally nest in large rural gardens. They sing only until early June, after which they are silent and very hard to see; they depart south for Africa in August or September.

Black Redstart *Phoenicurus ochruros* 14cm, 5.5in

In Britain, this close relative of the Common Redstart is found mainly in urban areas, preferring to nest amidst the hubbub of industrial sites (indeed, it originally colonized Britain via derelict bombsites following the Second World War). On mainland Europe, it behaves quite differently, preferring to live on the outskirts of small towns and villages, especially in more hilly areas with rocky terrain.

In flight, males (which are darker and smarter looking than females) show a pale wing patch. They are often detected by their distinctive song, which has a metallic quality like ball bearings being banged together.

Black Redstarts are partial migrants, heading away from their breeding areas in autumn and often spending the winter on the coasts or elsewhere near water.

Right: *As its name suggests, the Black Redstart is a more or less sooty black (or dark grey) bird with a rufous tail, often seen as it flicks it up and down.*

Redstart *Phoenicurus phoenicurus* 14cm, 5.5in

Usually associated with oak woods and valleys in the heart of the countryside, the Redstart may occasionally visit gardens, usually those near extensive areas of broad-leaved woodland. It is a summer visitor, returning in April or early May and departing again in the autumn, to spend the winter in West Africa.

The name Redstart derives from an Anglo-Saxon word *steort*, meaning tail (as the English language changed after the Norman Conquest, the original meaning became lost, and the word corrupted into 'start').

They nest in holes in trees or stone walls, laying five to seven bluish eggs, which hatch two weeks later. The young, which resemble the females, fledge two weeks afterwards, and are sometimes followed by a second brood.

Left: *Females are less easy to identify, appearing plain brown in colour, until you see their bright orange-red tail.*

Right: *With his smart red, black and grey plumage, the male Redstart is unmistakable.*

Whitethroat *Sylvia communis* 14cm, 5.5in

One of the commonest summer visitors to Britain and Europe, the Whitethroat is a member of the same group of warblers as the Blackcap and Garden Warbler. It is, however, less likely to be seen in gardens than its relatives, preferring scrubby areas with brambles or gorse on which it can perch.

In the late 1960s, Whitethroats underwent a serious population crash, when drought in the Sahel Zone of Western Africa meant that more than nine out of ten failed to return to breed the following spring. Fortunately, the species has made a full recovery, and its scratchy song can be heard from April onwards in suitable habitat. In autumn it may be seen in gardens, especially feeding on berries to stoke up fuel reserves before migration.

Right: *Whitethroats are identified by their brownish upperparts (with chestnut on the wing).*

Right:
They have pale underparts and a distinctive white throat from which the species gets its name.

Firecrest *Regulus ignicapillus* 9cm, 3.5in

Along with its close relative the Goldcrest, this is Britain and Europe's smallest species of bird. At just 9 cm (3.5 inches) long, and weighing just 5 grams (one-fifth of an ounce), it seems a miracle that a bird so small can survive, yet it does.

Firecrests can be told apart from their commoner relative by their much more colourful plumage.

In Britain, the Firecrest is a rare breeding bird, confined to southern counties, though its range may expand northwards thanks to global warming. In Europe, the species is more common, though less likely to be found in gardens than the Goldcrest, as it prefers mixed woodland. In winter, Firecrests often head for milder areas near water and may occasionally be seen in gardens.

Right: *Firecrests have a distinctive black-and-white face pattern, and rich orange patch on the flanks.*

Willow Tit *Parus montanus* 11.5cm, 4.5in

Distinguished from the Marsh Tit only at the end of the nineteenth century, the Willow Tit remains one of our most enigmatic breeding species. It is widely, though very thinly, distributed across England and Wales, and in recent years the population has dropped and the range contracted, for no very obvious reason.

It may visit birdtables close to damp wooded habitats, but is far less common in gardens than the Marsh Tit.

They lay six to nine pale eggs, which hatch after two weeks. Like most tits, they have only one brood.

Left: *Willow Tits nest in holes in trees, excavating their own hole in a rotting stump.*

Right: *Willow Tit can be told apart from the very similar Marsh Tit in a number of ways: its bulkier, 'bull-necked' appearance, pale patch on the wing, and sooty (not glossy) cap.*

Golden Oriole *Oriolus oriolus* 24cm, 9.5in

This stunning yellow-and-black bird is surely one of Europe's most beautiful species; yet because of its shy and retiring habits is rarely seen, even in areas where it is quite common. It is widely distributed throughout mainland Europe and may breed in large wooded gardens, but in Britain it is mainly confined to large plantations of trees such as alders and poplars. In recent years, the British population has grown, but it remains a rare and localized breeding bird.

Golden Orioles arrive back from Africa from late April (Europe) to mid-May (Britain).

Right: *Seen well, the male, with his gaudy golden-yellow plumage and black wings, is unmistakable, but females and juveniles are much duller, being mainly green in colour, and can be confused with Green Woodpecker on poor views.*

Tree Sparrow *Passer montanus* 14cm, 5.5in

Once a relatively familiar farmland bird, occasionally visiting gardens in order to feed, the Tree Sparrow has suffered a catastrophic population decline in the last few decades, largely due to changes in farming methods, which have reduced food supplies. In areas where the species still survives, garden feeding is a vital way to maintain a healthy population.

Right: *A chocolate brown (rather than grey) cap, pale collar and distinctive white spot behind the ear.*

Unlike the more familiar House Sparrow, both sexes of the Tree Sparrow are the same, superficially resembling the male of their cousin.

They breed from April onwards, nesting in holes in trees or walls. They can also be persuaded to use nestboxes and will raise several broods.

Above: *They are resident breeders, forming flocks with other sparrows, finches and buntings during the winter.*

Brambling *Fringilla montifringilla* 15.5cm, 6in

This colourful and attractive finch breeds mainly in the far north of Europe, where its range partly overlaps with that of its close relative the Chaffinch. In Britain and most of mainland Europe, it is primarily a winter visitor, arriving in autumn. Some years may see huge numbers, while in other winters it can be relatively scarce, depending on the availability of beech mast, its favourite food.

Bramblings are largely confined to woods in winter, but may be tempted to visit gardens, especially where there is a good range of seeds from trees available. They also sometimes feed at birdtables. Bramblings usually depart north in April, returning again in September or October.

Left: *Both sexes show a white rump in flight.*

Right: *The male Brambling is very distinctive, with dark head, pale yellowish bill and striking rusty-orange plumage. The female is less bright.*

Serin *Serinus serinus* 11cm, 4in

Europe's smallest finch is a common sight in gardens and villages throughout the Continent, but in Britain it is still a very rare visitor, which only occasionally breeds in southern counties. Listen out for the distinctive, tinkling, metallic song, often delivered from an overhead wire or post.

Serins have spread northwards in recent years and with a little help from global warming may well cross the Channel more regularly in the future. On the Continent they often breed in conifer hedges in gardens, laying three to five eggs. The young hatch two weeks later and fledge two weeks after that.

The Serin is a partial migrant, wintering mainly around the Mediterranean Sea.

Right: *Given good views, its small size, bright yellow throat and upper breast, and lack of black distinguish it from the larger Siskin. Females are less bright, but share the same cheeky demeanour.*

Linnet *Carduelis cannabina* 14cm, 5.5in

Once a common and familiar bird of mixed and arable farmland, the Linnet has suffered a rapid and serious decline in recent years – a fate it shares with many other species of seed-eating bird. The problem is that modern farming methods fail to leave seed for the birds to eat in winter.

Outside the breeding season, however, both males and females are the quintessential 'little brown jobs', though their 'jizz' and distinctive twittering call should make them easy to identify.

In recent years, they have begun to visit gardens more regularly, where they can find a welcome oasis of food, enabling them to survive the deprivations of their usual habitat. They are most likely to be seen in gardens in autumn and winter, often in flocks.

Right: *In breeding plumage, the male Linnet is very distinctive, sporting a pink forehead and bright pink patches on his breast.*

Redpoll *Carduelis cabaret / C. flammea* 12cm, 4.5in

The 'Redpoll' has recently been split into several separate species, including the Lesser Redpoll (*C. cabaret*), found in Britain and northwest Europe, and the Mealy Redpoll (*C. flammea*), a larger, much paler bird, found in Scandinavia and northern Europe. Occasionally, 'Mealies' will head south in numbers and may be seen in Britain in winter.

Young birds lack the red and are basically small streaky finches, with few obvious distinguishing features.

Redpolls form feeding flocks during the autumn and winter and often associate with their close relative, the Siskin. Both prefer to feed in trees such as alders, often near water, but Redpolls do occasionally visit gardens, even coming to birdtables and feeders. During the breeding season, they prefer woodlands and are rarely seen in gardens.

Right: *As their name suggests, Redpolls have a distinctive red patch on the forehead, which, if seen well, is diagnostic of this species.*

Hawfinch *Coccothraustes coccothraustes* 18cm, 7in

Britain's largest species of finch, the Hawfinch also sports one of the most powerful bills of any small bird, able to exert enough pressure to crack cherrystones. Yet this is rarely seen, as the Hawfinch is very shy, usually avoiding observation by staying high in the tops of mature trees.

Yet, in some places, Hawfinches are regular visitors to gardens, where they have been observed feeding, bathing and especially drinking, since they need plenty of water to help them to digest their dry food.

Hawfinches can be told apart from any other garden bird by their massive bill, bull-necked posture and dark face mask, which gives them a permanently surprised appearance. The only potential confusion species is the female Bullfinch, but she is much duller in colour.

Above: *The plumage is a mixture of pinkish brown, grey and buff, with black on the wings.*

Yellowhammer *Emberiza citrinella* 16.5cm, 6.5in

Despite its curious name, this attractive bunting does not have a hammer-like song or habits (its name derives from an Old German word meaning small bird). It is a typical bird of rural Britain and Europe, but, like so many seed-eating species, it has suffered from changes in farming methods and is now absent from many former haunts.

It is not a typical garden species, but, like several other finches and buntings, it has learned to adapt in recent years, and may visit gardens in order to find seeds when there are food shortages in the surrounding countryside. In spring and summer, you may also hear its distinctive song, supposed to sound like 'a-little-bit-of-bread-and-no-cheeeese'.

Left and above: *The Yellowhammer is easily identified by its bright yellow head (duller on the female) and streaky brown, black and chestnut plumage.*

Reed Bunting *Emberiza schoeniclus* 15.5cm, 6in

This handsome member of the bunting family used to be a rare visitor to gardens, but, like several of its relatives, it has become a more frequent sight in recent years. This is despite, or perhaps because of, the fact that this period has coincided with a rapid population decline in the wider countryside: it may be that food shortages have forced the birds to seek food farther afield.

In winter, Reed Buntings feed mainly on seeds and will regularly visit bird-tables and feeders, even in gardens some distance from their usual reedbed haunts.

Left and above: *Although the black head of the breeding male (above) is distinctive, in autumn and winter males and females (left) both look fairly nondescript at first sight. Closer views reveal a streaky bird rather like a bright female sparrow, with obvious white outer tail feathers in flight, and sometimes traces of the striped head pattern.*

FLYOVER SPECIES

Raptors

Day-flying birds of prey are well known for their soaring capabilities and may often be seen flying overhead. As well as the typical garden visitors (**Kestrel** and **Sparrowhawk**), you may also see Britain and Europe's largest common bird of prey, the **Buzzard** (*Buteo buteo*).

The **Hobby** (*Falco subbuteo*) is a small, slender, fast-flying falcon, which is a summer visitor to southern Britain and mainland Europe. It is dark, almost Swift-like in appearance and is extremely agile, twisting and turning to hunt flying insects such as dragonflies, or even small birds such as House Martins.

In some urban areas, the larger **Peregrine** (*Falco peregrinus*) is becoming more common. Once persecuted and poisoned, the species has made a comeback in recent years, and is found in many cities, where it feeds on unsuspecting pigeons.

In spring and autumn, you may be lucky enough to have an **Osprey** (*Pandion haliaetus*) fly over your garden, especially if you live near a large area of water such as a lake, reservoir or flooded gravel pit. Ospreys breed in Scotland and Scandinavia, but winter in Africa.

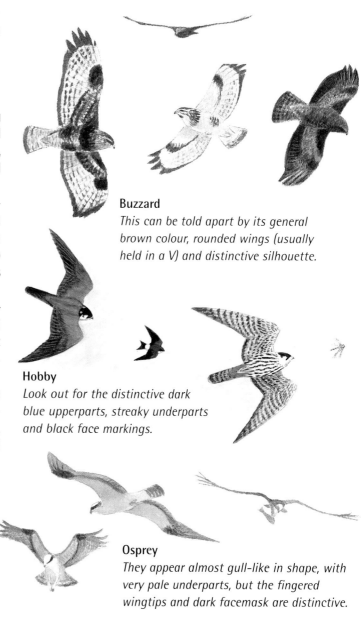

Buzzard
This can be told apart by its general brown colour, rounded wings (usually held in a V) and distinctive silhouette.

Hobby
Look out for the distinctive dark blue upperparts, streaky underparts and black face markings.

Osprey
They appear almost gull-like in shape, with very pale underparts, but the fingered wingtips and dark facemask are distinctive.

Peregrine
Look out for a solidly-built, large falcon, with broad-based, pointed wings and a deep chest.

Ducks, Geese and Swans

If your garden is near water, you may well see wildfowl flying overhead. Some, especially ducks, can be frustratingly difficult to identify, but given good views you should be able to do so.

The most usual species of duck seen over gardens are **Mallard**, **Tufted Duck** (*Aythya fuligula*) and **Pochard** (*Aythya ferina*), though many other kinds of dabbling and diving duck are also possible. The best way to identify ducks in flight is to look out for distinctive field-marks such as wingbars.

So-called 'grey' geese are also an identification headache. The most likely species to be encountered is **Greylag Goose** (*Anser anser*), which has established a thriving feral population in parts of Britain and Europe.

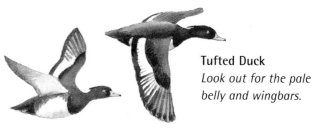

Tufted Duck
Look out for the pale belly and wingbars.

Pochard
They appear very pale, with a dark head and belly.

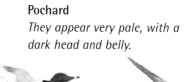

Canada Geese (*Branta canadensis*) are a familiar sight over much of Britain nowadays and, if you see a goose flying over your garden, it is fairly likely to be this species. **Barnacle Goose** (*Branta leucopsis*) is another possibility, while **White-fronted Goose** (*Anser albifrons*) may also be seen in hard winter weather. A feral species, **Egyptian Goose** (*Alopochen aegyptiacus*), is now expanding its range, and is easily identified by broad white patches on its wings.

Perhaps the easiest kind of wildfowl to identify is the **Mute Swan** (*Cygnus olor*): huge, white and unmistakable, unless you live near an area where the two species of wild swans are present.

Canada Goose and Barnacle Goose
Feral geese are much more common than they used to be, with several species likely to be seen.

Mute Swan, Whooper Swan, Bewick's Swan
All three species of swan are possible flyover species, but the Mute Swan is far more likely than the two winter visitors.

Gulls

Gulls are a common sight over many gardens, especially those near the coast, lakes or reservoirs, in areas of arable farmland. Even in towns and cities, winter flocks of gulls find rich pickings amongst our waste.

By far the commonest species almost everywhere (except on the coast) is **Black-headed Gull** (*Larus ridibundus*), which outside the breeding season lacks the distinctive brown hood. It can be identified by its small size and pointed wings. **Common Gull** (*Larus canus*) is another frequent winter visitor inland, and can be distinguished by its slightly larger size and much more rounded wings.

Common Gull
A relatively common bird inland, especially in winter.

Herring Gull
Less common in or over gardens, but frequent near the sea.

Black-headed Gull
The classic inland gull, and a frequent visitor to gardens, mainly outside the breeding season.

Larger gulls include **Herring Gull** (*Larus argentatus*) and **Lesser Black-backed Gull** (*Larus fuscus*), both far commoner inland than they used to be. These two species now breed on buildings in major cities, so may be seen all year around. Both are much larger than Common or Black-headed Gulls and Herring has pale grey upperparts with black wingtips, while Lesser Black-backed has much darker, almost black upper wings. **Great Black-backed Gull** (*Larus marinus*) is far less frequent inland. It is huge, with completely black upperwings and a massive head and bill.

Lesser Black-backed Gull
An increasingly common bird inland, especially near large cities.

Great Black-backed Gull
The rarest of the five common gulls inland, but may be seen flying over.

Others

Almost any other species that occurs in the region may sometimes fly over gardens and there have been extraordinary records of waders, rare songbirds and even seabirds well inland. Apart from those mentioned, the most likely species to fly over gardens include **Common Tern** (*Sterna hirundo*), an elegant bird which now nests inland far more than it used to; **Sand Martin** (*Riparia riparia*) and songbirds such as **Skylark** (*Alauda arvensis*) or **Meadow Pipit** (*Anthus pratensis*). These may be hard to identify, though their distinctive calls may help.

Common Tern
This summer visitor may be seen passing overhead.

Skylark
Less common than it used to be, but may be heard passing over in autumn.

Meadow Pipit
Listen out for the thin 'sip' call of Meadow Pipits on early mornings in autumn.

Sand Martin
Look out for this species in March and April, when it returns to breed.

Plants to Attract Birds

Choosing plants that will attract birds to your garden is not an exact science: opinions do differ as to which particular plants are best for which birds. You also need to take into account other factors, such as the soil in your garden, the prevailing weather conditions and the size and shape of your garden.

You may also want to decide what proportion of your garden should be allowed to 'go wild', what proportion you wish to keep as open lawn and flower beds, and whether you are planning a complete redesign or simply tinkering at the edges.

A typical garden consists of several interconnected 'mini-habitats', including a lawn, flower-beds, shrubberies and mature trees. You may also have a pond and 'wild area', or if you have not already done so, want to create these.

It is also worth making an 'audit' of the plants that you already have and their attractiveness to birds. You can rate them according to whether they do any of the following:
- Provide food directly for birds (e.g. seeds, berries, fruit).
- Attract insects and invertebrates on which birds can feed.
- Give shelter for roosting birds.
- Provide suitable places for nesting.

Ideally, you should try to plant a range of different plants for different uses, concentrating mainly (though certainly not exclusively) on native varieties, as these tend to attract the most insects. For example, more than 300 different kinds of insects and invertebrates live on a typical oak tree, whereas an imported tree, such as the Sycamore, may only support a handful of different species.

Try to have a combination of different plants, including larger trees and hedges (if your garden is large enough to support them), berry-bearing bushes and shrubs, climbing plants in which birds can build their nests, seed-bearing flowering plants, and, if possible, a rough area in which you have let your garden go a little bit wild.

Try also, if possible, to create different levels in your garden, to suit different species and their feeding methods. For example, species such as the Dunnock tend to forage on the ground or in a low flower bed, whereas others, like the Blackcap, prefer to feed a metre or more above the ground.

Lack of space may be a problem, especially if you live in an urban area. With a little imagination, you can maximise the available area, by planting climbers, for example.

Most of these plants will grow in the 'typical' garden, but may not 'work' for gardens in a more unusual situation. If your garden is at high altitude, near the coast, in the extreme north or west of Britain, or exposed to the elements, you will need to consider planting a range of hardy plants suited to your situation. Shelter is vital if the garden is exposed to high winds, and fast-growing non-native plants may work better than native varieties.

Left and above: *Native varieties such as Honeysuckle (above) and non-native species such as Buddleia (left) or 'butterfly bush' can be planted together to provide plenty of food.*

Right: *A classic British scene: a Blue Tit perched on a Hawthorn bush in autumn.*

Trees and Hedges

A large, mature tree, such as an Oak, brings enormous benefits to your garden, but, let's face it, if you haven't already got one, you may have to wait rather a long time after planting an acorn before seeing the benefits. Smaller trees, such as Willow and Alder, are also excellent for birds, and are fast-growing in comparison. Fruit trees, such as Crab Apple and Apple, also grow quickly, and attract insects as well as providing fruit in autumn.

Hedgerows are also excellent for birds and provide an attractive feature as well. Privet and Laurel are excellent, and cypresses, despite their bad press, are a favourite amongst many birds, especially Greenfinches, as they provide plenty of places to roost and nest. Do, however, be sensitive to your neighbours' needs.

Ideally you should avoid ornamental species such as Sycamore and Flowering Cherry, as they support few insects.

Apple *(below)*

There are many cultivated varieties of apple, which provide delicious fruit for us as well as for the birds. An added bonus is that in spring the blossom attracts lots of insects, ideal for feeding hungry young birds.

Alder *(below)*

Alders are a favourite source of food for many species, especially Siskin and Redpoll, which love the catkins in spring and seed cones in autumn and winter. Alders grow best beside running water.

Cypress (*above*)

The dreaded 'Leylandii' cypress is the subject of more disputes between neighbours than any other garden plant, owing to its incredibly fast rate of growth, which can soon overshadow your or your neighbour's garden. This can be turned to your advantage, however, if you are in a hurry to provide cover for roosting and nesting in your garden.

Hawthorn (*above*)

The Hawthorn, or, as it is known in old country folklore, the may-tree, is ideal for planting, either as a single bush or as part of a hedgerow. Its blossom will attract plenty of insects in spring and summer and in autumn it produces a mass of berries, which attract all kinds of birds including thrushes, pigeons and, if you are lucky, even Waxwings.

Oak (*right*)

The Oak is more or less the perfect tree for birds – and indeed most other wildlife! It attracts plenty of different varieties of insects and other invertebrates, especially caterpillars, on which birds can feed themselves and their young. It also offers plenty of suitable sites for nesting birds such as woodpeckers and other hole-nesters. In autumn, the bumper crop of acorns is ideal for Nuthatches and Jays, many of which travel from continental Europe to feed here. If you have a mature Oak tree in your garden, consider yourself lucky!

Bushes and Shrubs

These are an excellent and varied habitat for garden birds, providing plenty of food and good places to shelter, roost and build nests. There are hundreds of varieties on the market, including varieties such as Cotoneaster and Barberry (great for berries); Broom and Guelder Rose. Favourites amongst gardeners and birds alike are Buddleia, Elder, Firethorn (Pyracantha) and Holly.

Many of these plants provide food in two ways, at different times of the year: in spring, blossom that attracts insects, and, in autumn, berries.

Berries provide much-needed energy at a crucial time of year when other food resources are getting scarce, and are especially popular amongst thrushes, pigeons, Starlings and several species of warbler. The plants benefit by getting their seed spread around; while the birds get a free meal.

Buddleia *(above)*

Known popularly as the 'butterfly bush', and with good reason: in late summer your Buddleia will be covered in huge purple flowers which attract a wide range of insects, including many butterflies. As well as common species such as Small Tortoiseshell and Comma, you may also see migrants such as Red Admiral and Painted Lady. In turn, this means that there will be plenty of caterpillars for birds such as tits to feed their hungry young. Buddleias love the sun, and will grow on most fertile soils. They can grow very quickly, so make sure that you prune them.

Elder *(above)*

The Elder is one of our most familiar native shrubs and trees, found in hedgerows everywhere. It is a veritable treasure-house for the birds, providing nectar to attract insects in summer and crops of luscious purplish-black berries in the autumn. These attract a whole range of birds, especially Blackbirds and other thrushes, and are also a firm favourite with Wood Pigeons. Here, a Blue Tit seems interested. Elders provide plenty of cover for nesting and, as an added bonus, you can make delicious wines from both the flowers and the berries.

Firethorn *(left)*

The various species of this exotic garden plant provide plenty of berries in autumn and early winter, and, as a result, attract the usual berry-loving birds: thrushes (including Blackbird, Fieldfare and Redwing), Wood Pigeon and, if you are very fortunate, Waxwing.

Holly *(right)*

The classic plant of the Christmas season is excellent for birds, as its berries mature later than those of many other plants, providing food in late autumn and winter when the birds need it most. The Holly's dense, evergreen foliage also provides excellent cover for roosting and nesting. Mistle Thrushes, in particular, love the berries and will often defend a holly bush for the whole of the winter period against all-comers, fighting off any bird which dares to try to take its precious crop. This can be a fascinating sight to observe if you are lucky enough to see it in your own garden.

Flowering Plants

Birds love flowering plants just as much as we do, but not for their aesthetic quality; they produce two very valuable food resources for birds: nectar and seeds. They have the added bonus of attracting plenty of insects, especially caterpillars, which many species (especially Blue and Great Tits) require in order to feed their young.

Try to go for native varieties such as Foxglove, Red Campion, Primrose and Wild Poppy, though non-native varieties also attract a wide variety of insects and provide seeds for the birds. Sunflowers are another favourite amongst birds and gardeners alike, for their seeds and for their large, yellow flowers.

Cornflower *(below, background)*

This annual plant grows quickly and looks great, especially if you plant the seeds in a sunny, well-drained flowerbed. It attracts loads of insects and, once it has flowered, the seeds are loved by tits and finches.

Corn Poppy *(above, foreground)*

The classic red poppy adds a splash of colour to any flower bed and flowers during May to July, attracting a host of insects. Afterwards, the seed heads are an excellent source of food, especially for finches and sparrows.

Lavender *(left)*

There are many varieties of Lavender, all providing that distinctive scent so beloved of aromatherapists. Insects love it too, bees and butterflies in particular. In autumn, the seed-heads attract finches.

Marsh Marigold (above)

This lovely perennial plant grows best around the edge of a pond, producing clusters of bright golden flowers in the spring. It requires boggy ground or very shallow water, and flowers very early in the spring, often in April if the weather is suitable.

Meadow Buttercup (above)

The classic meadow flower produces its yellow blooms from spring to autumn and always adds a splash of colour to a garden, especially if you have allowed part of your lawn to 'go wild' as a hay meadow. It attracts all kinds of tiny insects.

Primrose (above)

This widespread wild flower has long been cultivated and adapted to grow in our gardens. It forms attractive clumps of flowers, especially on a rockery. In spring, it plays host to the usual insects, while in autumn the seeds attract plenty of birds such as finches. Primroses have lovely yellow flowers, though garden varieties may come in a wider range of colours.

Sunflower (above)

This huge and stunning-looking plant grows incredibly quickly and is an ideal way to get young children fired with enthusiasm for the joys of gardening. The huge, dark-centred yellow flowers attract loads of insects and, after flowering, the seed-heads will provide a cheap supply of sunflower seeds for your feeders. A real favourite amongst all seed-eating birds.

Climbing Plants

Climbing plants, such as Clematis, Honeysuckle, Ivy, Hydrangea and even grapevines, have three advantages, especially if you have a small garden where space is at a premium. First, they grow relatively quickly and will become an established part of your garden; secondly, they provide plenty of cover, especially for nesting birds; and thirdly, they look great. Honeysuckle and Ivy also provide berries, while all have lovely flowers that attract insects in spring and summer.

Clematis (below)

Clematis has always been a favourite plant amongst gardeners and with good reason: it grows rapidly to cover a wall or fence and looks lovely, even when it is not in flower. Birds love it, too, especially those, such as Blackbirds, that require dense cover to provide a secluded place for nesting.

Honeysuckle (above)

Another gardeners' favourite, and for the birds too. The flowers produce nectar that attracts insects, so that small birds, such as warblers, may come to feed on both the nectar and the insects. The berries are also excellent fuel for warblers as they prepare to migrate, and later in the season for finches and thrushes.

Ivy *(right)*

Along with the Holly, this other plant of the Christmas season comes in many different varieties, all adept at climbing up trees, walls, piles of logs and fences and providing plenty of thick cove.. This is ideal for nesting birds, such as the Wren, the flowers attract many insects in autumn and the berries provide a source of food in winter for thrushes and other berry-loving species.

Lawns

Don't forget that as well as shrubberies and flower beds, lawns and rockeries can also be excellent places for birds to feed. Thrushes, Blackbirds, Starlings and Pied Wagtails are particularly partial to probing or picking on short turf, while, if you are very lucky, a Green Woodpecker may visit to your lawn to forage for ants.

Ground-feeding birds will benefit if you turn part of your lawn into a seasonal wildflower meadow, allowing the grass to grow longer than usual and planting a variety of wild meadow flowers.

Below: *If you live in the country your lawn may become a favourite haunt of Pheasants such as this female.*

Wilderness Area

If you are feeling brave, you may want to convert part of your garden to a wilderness area. This does not mean letting it simply 'go wild', but involves hard work and planning to get the best out of it.

For many gardeners it also means fighting their in-built prejudice against 'weeds' such as Teasel, Bramble, Stinging Nettle and Dandelion.

For advice on how to create a wildlife garden, turn to an excellent book *Chris Packham's Back Garden Nature Reserve* (see *Further Reading*).

Bramble *(above)*

The common bramble may not be the most attractive garden plant, but it provides great cover for nesting birds such as the Dunnock and, in autumn, the blackberry crop will provide a free meal for a whole variety of hungry birds, including Whitethroat, Blackbird and Song Thrush. And, if the birds leave anything, you can make a nice pie, or even some blackberry jam to spread on your toast during the winter and remind you of the birds of autumn!

Common Nettle *(left)*

Stinging Nettles in a garden? Am I mad?! Well, no, because nettles attract a host of caterpillars and other small insects and, in autumn, the plant produces plenty of seeds. Stick it in a corner where you can't see it from the kitchen window. If you are really squeamish, or have young children who may be stung, there are rare stingless varieties available!

Cow Parsley *(right)*

This classic hedgerow plant is one of the quintessential sights of the British rural summer. From late April to early July, it produces plenty of off-white flowers, which later turn into small fruits that birds love.

Teasel *(above)*

A classic plant of disturbed areas of open ground, the teasel produces wonderful spiky seed-heads, which one species in particular is adapted to exploit. The Goldfinch has evolved a very sharp bill in order to remove the Teasel's seeds from its heads; plant them and you are in for an autumn treat.

Yarrow *(above)*

This pretty, delicate plant is a common feature across Britain in hedgerows and fields. It will also adapt well to gardens, especially if planted in a sunny area on well-drained soil. The seed heads are excellent for tits, sparrows and finches and, in spring, it also attracts plenty of insects.

Useful Addresses

Organizations

The Wildlife Trusts
The Kiln
Waterside
Mather Road
Newark NG24 1WT
Tel: 0870 036 7711
Fax: 0870 036 0101
Email: enquiry@wildlifetrusts.org
Web: www.wildlifetrusts.org
The Wildlife Trusts is the UK's leading voluntary organization working on all aspects of wildlife protection and people involvement. They manage almost 2,500 nature reserves throughout the UK, have more than 600,000 members and receive support from over 22,000 volunteers every year. Members receive local magazines and information, and the award-winning UK magazine, *Natural World*, three times a year.

The Wildlife Trusts' Information Service
The Wildlife Trusts will try to answer any queries from members of the public on all aspects of wildlife conservation across the UK. Either get in touch with your local Wildlife Trust, or contact the UK office (details above).

Wildlife Watch
(Contact details as above)
Email: watch@wildlife-trusts.cix.co.uk
Web: www.wildlife-watch.org
Wildlife Watch is the children's club and junior branch of The Wildlife Trusts and has 60,000 members. Members receive three magazines with articles and ideas, three large posters with tips on wildlife watching and the chance to join other children once a month to discover local wildlife.

BTO (British Trust for Ornithology)
The National Centre for Ornithology
The Nunnery
Thetford
Norfolk IP24 2PU
Tel: 01842 750 050
Fax: 01842 750 030
Email: info@bto.org
Web: www.bto.org
The BTO offers birdwatchers the opportunity to learn more about birds by taking part in surveys such as the Garden BirdWatch or the Nest Record Scheme. BTO members also receive a bi-monthly magazine, BTO News.

CJ Wildbird Foods Ltd
The Rea
Upton Magna
Shrewsbury SY4 4UR
Tel: 0800 731 2820 (Freephone)
Fax: 01743 709 504
Email: enquiries@birdfood.co.uk
Web: www.birdfood.co.uk
CJ Wildbird Foods is Britain's leading supplier of birdfeeders and foodstuffs, via mail order. The company sponsors the BTO Garden BirdWatch survey and also produce a free handbook of garden feeding, containing advice on feeding garden birds, and a catalogue of products.

Haith's
65 Park Street
Cleethorpes
Lincolnshire DN35 7NF
Tel: 0800 298 7054 (Freephone)
Fax: 01472 242 883
Email: enquiries@haiths.com
Web: www.haiths.com
Established in 1937, Haith's are committed to producing high quality wild bird foods, bird feeders, accessories, gifts and much more. The company supports the vital work of The Wildlife Trusts across the UK through the sale of Bill Oddie's Natural Choice birdfood and other products.

RSPB (Royal Society for the Protection of Birds)
The Lodge
Sandy
Bedfordshire SG19 2DL
Tel: 01767 680 551
Fax: 01767 692 365
Email: bird@rspb.demon.co.uk
Web: www.rspb.org.uk
The RSPB is Britain's leading bird conservation organization, with over one million members. It runs more than 100 bird reserves up and down the country, and has a national network of members' groups. Members receive four copies of *Birds* magazine each year, while new members receive a gift on joining. The junior arm of the RSPB, the Young Ornithologists Club (YOC) is for members up to the age of 16.

RSPB Enquiry Unit
(Contact details as above)
The RSPB Enquiry Unit answers written or telephone queries on anything to do with birds. The phone lines are open from Monday to Friday, 9 a.m.–5.15 p.m.

Subbuteo Natural History Books Ltd
The Rea
Upton Magna
Shrewsbury SY4 4UR
Tel: 0870 010 9700
Fax: 0870 010 9699
Email: info@wildlifebooks.com
Web: www.wildlifebooks.com
Subbuteo Books provides a fast, helpful and reliable mail order service for books on birds and other aspects of natural history, including those on garden birds. Free catalogue available on request. With every purchase, Subbuteo gives a five per cent donation to support the work of The Wildlife Trusts.

Wildfowl and Wetlands Trust
Slimbridge
Gloucestershire GL2 7BT
Tel: 01453 891 900
Fax: 01453 890 827
Email: enquiries@wwt.org.uk
Web: www.wwt.org.uk
The Wildfowl and Wetlands Trust is the largest international wetland conservation charity in the UK, and is supported by over 139,000 members.

Wildsounds
Dept ABG
Cross Street
Salthouse
Norfolk NR25 7XH
Tel: 01263 741 100
Fax: 01263 741 838
Email: isales@wildsounds.com
Web: www.wildsounds.co.uk
Wildsounds is Britain's leading supplier of birdsong tapes and CDs. They also stock a range of Teach Yourself products, particularly useful for the beginner.

Magazines

BBC Wildlife
Available monthly from newsagents, or by subscription from:
BBC Wildlife Subscriptions
PO Box 279
Sittingbourne
Kent ME9 8DF
Tel: 01795 414 718
Web: www.bbcbritishwildlifemagazine.com

Birdwatch
Available monthly from larger newsagents, or by subscription from:
Warners
West Street
Bourne
Lincolnshire PE10 9PH
Tel: 01778 392 027
Web: www.birdwatch.co.uk

Bird Watching
Available monthly from larger newsagents, or by subscription from:
EMAP Active
Bretton Court
Bretton
Peterborough PE3 8DZ
Tel: 0845 601 1356

British Birds
Available monthly by subscription only from:
The Banks
Mountfield
Robertsbridge
East Sussex TN32 5JY
Tel: 01580 882 039
Web: www.britishbirds.co.uk

Help protect the UK's wildlife by joining
The Wildlife Trusts on 0870 0367711
or online at www.wildlifetrusts.org

Further Reading

Baines, Chris
How to Make a Wildlife Garden
Frances Lincoln, 2000

Baker, Nick
Nick Baker's British Wildlife
New Holland, 2003

Beddard, Roy
The Garden Bird Year
New Holland, 2001

Burton, John A.
The Ultimate Birdfeeder Handbook
New Holland, 2005

Cannon, Andrew
The Garden Bird Watch Handbook
British Trust for Ornithology, 2000

Couzens, Dominic
The Complete Back Garden Birdwatcher
New Holland, 2005

De Feu, Chris
Nestboxes
British Trust for Ornithology, 1993

Golley, Mark
Birdwatcher's Pocket Field Guide
New Holland, 2003

Golley, Mark, Moss, Stephen and Daly, David
The Complete Garden Bird Book
New Holland, 2001

Golley, Mark
The Complete Garden Wildlife Book
New Holland, 2006

Hammond, Nicholas (Series Editor)
The Wildlife Trusts Guide to Birds
New Holland, 2002

Hammond, Nicholas (Series Editor)
The Wildlife Trusts Guide to Garden Wildlife
New Holland, 2002

Hammond, Nicholas (Series Editor)
The Wildlife Trusts Handbook of Garden Wildlife
New Holland, 2002

Moss, Stephen
The Private Life of Birds
New Holland, 2006

Moss, Stephen
A Birdwatcher's Guide: How to Birdwatch
New Holland, 2003

Moss, Stephen and Cottridge, David
Attracting Birds to your Garden
New Holland, 2000

Oddie, Bill
Bill Oddie's Birds of Britain and Ireland
New Holland, 2002

Oddie, Bill
Bill Oddie's Introduction to Birdwatching
New Holland, 2002

Packham, Chris
Chris Packham's Back Garden Nature Reserve
New Holland, 2001

Soper, Tony
The Bird Table Book
David and Charles, 1992

Ward, Mark
Birdwatcher's Guide: Bird Identification and Fieldcraft
New Holland, 2005

Tick List

Regular Species

Grey Heron *Ardea cinerea*	❏	Garden Warbler *Sylvia borin*	❏
Mallard *Anas platyrhynchos*	❏	Blackcap *Sylvia atricapilla*	❏
Sparrowhawk *Accipiter nisus*	❏	Chiffchaff *Phylloscopus collybita*	❏
Kestrel *Falco tinnunculus*	❏	Willow Warbler *Phylloscopus trochilus*	❏
Pheasant *Phasianus colchicus*	❏	Goldcrest *Regulus regulus*	❏
Black-headed Gull *Larus ridibundus*	❏	Spotted Flycatcher *Muscicapa striata*	❏
Feral Pigeon *Columba livia*	❏	Long-tailed Tit *Aegithalos caudatus*	❏
Stock Dove *Columba oenas*	❏	Marsh Tit *Parus palustris*	❏
Wood Pigeon *Columba palumbus*	❏	Coal Tit *Parus ater*	❏
Collared Dove *Streptopelia decaocto*	❏	Blue Tit *Parus caeruleus*	❏
Tawny Owl *Strix aluco*	❏	Great Tit *Parus major*	❏
Swift *Apus apus*	❏	Nuthatch *Sitta europaea*	❏
Green Woodpecker *Picus viridis*	❏	Treecreeper *Certhia familiaris*	❏
Great Spotted Woodpecker *Dendrocopos major*	❏	Jay *Garrulus glandarius*	❏
Swallow *Hirundo rustica*	❏	Magpie *Pica pica*	❏
House Martin *Delichon urbica*	❏	Jackdaw *Corvus monedula*	❏
Pied Wagtail *Motacilla alba*	❏	Rook *Corvus frugilegus*	❏
Wren *Troglodytes troglodytes*	❏	Carrion/Hooded Crow *Corvus corone*	❏
Dunnock *Prunella modularis*	❏	Starling *Sturnus vulgaris*	❏
Robin *Erithacus rubecula*	❏	House Sparrow *Passer domesticus*	❏
Blackbird *Turdus merula*	❏	Chaffinch *Fringilla coelebs*	❏
Fieldfare *Turdus pilaris*	❏	Greenfinch *Carduelis chloris*	❏
Song Thrush *Turdus philomelos*	❏	Goldfinch *Carduelis carduelis*	❏
Redwing *Turdus iliacus*	❏	Siskin *Carduelis spinus*	❏
Mistle Thrush *Turdus viscivorus*	❏	Bullfinch *Pyrrhula pyrrhula*	❏

Unusal Species

White Stork *Ciconia ciconia* ❏

Red-legged Partridge *Alectoris rufa* ❏

Moorhen *Gallinula chloropus* ❏

Turtle Dove *Streptopelia turtur* ❏

Rose-ringed Parakeet *Psittacula krameri* ❏

Cuckoo *Cuculus canorus* ❏

Barn Owl *Tyto alba* ❏

Little Owl *Athene noctua* ❏

Kingfisher *Alcedo atthis* ❏

Hoopoe *Upupa epops* ❏

Wryneck *Jynx torquilla* ❏

Lesser Spotted Woodpecker *Dendrocopos minor* ❏

Yellow/Blue-headed Wagtail *Motacilla flava* ❏

Grey Wagtail *Motacilla cinerea* ❏

Waxwing *Bombycilla garrulus* ❏

Nightingale *Luscinia megarhynchos* ❏

Black Redstart *Phoenicurus ochruros* ❏

Redstart *Phoenicurus phoenicurus* ❏

Whitethroat *Sylvia communis* ❏

Firecrest *Regulus ignicapillus* ❏

Willow Tit *Parus montanus* ❏

Golden Oriole *Oriolus oriolus* ❏

Tree Sparrow *Passer montanus* ❏

Brambling *Fringilla montifringilla* ❏

Serin *Serinus serinus* ❏

Linnet *Carduelis cannabina* ❏

Redpoll *Carduelis cabaret/C. flammea* ❏

Hawfinch *Coccothraustes coccothraustes* ❏

Yellowhammer *Emberiza citrinella* ❏

Reed Bunting *Emberiza schoeniclus* ❏

Other Species

.... ❏

.... ❏

.... ❏

.... ❏

.... ❏

.... ❏

.... ❏

.... ❏

.... ❏

.... ❏

.... ❏

.... ❏

.... ❏

.... ❏

.... ❏

.... ❏

.... ❏

.... ❏

.... ❏

.... ❏

Index

Page numbers in **bold** refer to illustrations

Acknowledgements

At New Holland, I would like to thank Lorna Sharrock, for her tactful editing skills, and Jo Hemmings, for commissioning the book in the first place!

David Daly's delightful illustrations, and the photographs from a variety of Britain's top photographers including David Cottridge, have made it a lovely book to look at as well as, hopefully, useful and interesting to read. Also, thanks to Tim Sharrock for his rigorous and helpful copy editing.

Working with Charlie Dimmock and Chris Baines on the BBC2 television series *Charlie's Wildlife Gardens* enabled me to gain practical experience of the joys of digging a pond – or at least watching others do it! Chris's books and lectures on the subject of wildlife gardening continue to inspire me along with many others. Another great inspiration is Chris Whittles at CJ Wildbird Foods, who has probably done more than anyone else to encourage the feeding and care of garden birds.

My late mother, Kay Moss, first got me interested in gardens; and I like to think that some of her love of the subject has rubbed off on me. The same applies to my aunt and uncle, Sally and John Rose, whose garden is still a great pleasure. As always, my wife Suzanne has been an inspiration and a great practical help: may we continue to enjoy our garden birds for very many years to come.

Finally, I dedicate this book to my late grandmother, Edna Vale, who first showed me that feeding birds in your garden can bring a lifetime's pleasure and joy.

Stephen Moss

Publisher's Acknowledgements
All artwork by David Daly, with the exception of the following:
David Ashby: p30
Clive Byers: pp64(t), 84, 137(Peregrine, Hobby)
Sheila Hadley: p38
Stephen Message: p139 (Common Tern)
Wildlife Art Ltd: Cy Baker: pp29(t), 95; Robin Carter: pp22, 23, 24, 25

All photographs by David Cottridge, with the exception of the following:
Richard Brooks: p4(tl)
Gordon Langsbury: pp67, 80, 101(b)
Tim Loseby: pp9, 10, 14, 24, 31(t), 51, 56, 58(t), 83
Nature Photograhers: S.C. Bisserot: p142(b); Frank B. Blackburn: p98; T. D. Bonsall: p59(t); Brinsley Burbidge: pp148(b), 151(br);
Robin Bush: p146(t); Colin Carver: pp52, 74; Ron Croucher: p28; Geoff du Feu: pp96, 146(b); Chris Grey-Wilson: p41; Jean Hall: p26(b);
E. A. Janes: pp13(t), 32(b), 48; Philip Newman: p55; Paul Sterry: pp11, 26(tl), 42(b), 43, 49, 99(t), 143(tl), 148(t), 149(t), 150(b);
Roger Tidman: pp53, 59(b); Derek Washington: p147(tr)
Richard Revels: pp4(b), 26(tr), 27(b), 47, 99(bl), 141(t)
CJ Wildbird Foods: pp6, 17, 21
Alan Williams: Front cover, pp50, 68, 73, 84, 88, 89
Windrush Photos: Bill Coster: p54; Gordon Langsbury: Back cover, p91; Mark Lucas: p37(t); David Tipling: pp 4(tr), 151(bl)

With special thanks to CJ Wildbird Foods for supplying the photographs on pages 6, 17 and 21.